GREAT AMERICAN HOMES

HISTORIC CHARLESTON

BY SHIRLEY ABBOTT

HOUSES PHOTOGRAPHED BY PETER VITALÉ

ADDITIONAL PHOTOGRAPHY BY STEVEN MAYS

Printed exclusively for
CHARLESTON POST CARD CO. INC.
2136 Coker Avenue
Charleston, South Carolina
29412

Great American Homes was created and produced by Rebus, Inc. and published by Oxmoor House, Inc.

Rebus, Inc.

Publisher: Rodney Friedman
Editor: Charles L. Mee, Jr.
Picture Editor: Mary Z. Jenkins
Art Director: Ronald Gross
Managing Editor: Fredrica A. Harvey

Production: Paul Levin, Giga Communications, Inc.

Author: Shirley Abbott, executive editor at Rebus, Inc., was formerly the editor of *Horizon* magazine. She is the author of *Womenfolks: Growing Up Down South* and *The National Museum of American History*, about that branch of the Smithsonian Institution.

Photographers: Peter Vitale is a New York-based photographer whose work has appeared in *Architectural Digest*, *Interior Design*, and *House & Garden*. Steven Mays is chief photographer at Rebus, Inc.; his work appeared in the *Treasures of the World* series.

Consultant: Gene Waddell, director of the South Carolina Historical Society from 1976 to 1984, is now associate archivist at the Getty Center for the History of Art and the Humanities, Santa Monica, California. He has coauthored two books on American architectural history and is currently at work on a book about the architecture of Charleston.

Copyright © 1988 by Rebus, Inc.

Published by Oxmoor House, Inc.
Book Division of Southern Progress Corporation
P.O. Box 2463
Birmingham, AL 35201

All rights reserved. No part of this book may be reproduced, stored in a retrieval system or transmitted, in any form or by any means, electronic, mechanical, photocopying, recording or otherwise, without permission in writing from the publisher.

Library of Congress
Cataloging in Publication Data
Abbott, Shirley.
　Historic Charleston.

　(Great American homes)
　Includes index.
　1. Charleston (S.C.)—Dwellings. 2. Historic buildings—South Carolina—Charleston. 3. Architecture, Georgian—South Carolina—Charleston. I. Title. II. Series.
NA7238.C3A22　720′.9757′915　84-15505
ISBN 0-8487-0756-7

Cover: Roper House.

CONTENTS

FOREWORD 4

INTRODUCTION 6

CHAPTER 1
HEYWARD-WASHINGTON HOUSE: HOME OF THE BRAVE 18

PORTFOLIO
GRAND ENTRANCES 36

CHAPTER 2
MANIGAULT HOUSE: A CHARLESTON DYNASTY 50

PORTFOLIO
OBJECTS OF GRACE 68

CHAPTER 3
NATHANIEL RUSSELL HOUSE: A NEST OF ROSES 82

PORTFOLIO
FURNITURE IN THE BEST MANNER 102

CHAPTER 4
EDMONDSTON-ALSTON HOUSE: OLD TIMES AND OKRA SOUP 116

PORTFOLIO
AUDUBON IN CHARLESTON 128

CHAPTER 5
ROPER HOUSE: A VIEW TO THE CANARIES 142

PORTFOLIO
OUTLYING EDENS 160

ACKNOWLEDGMENTS AND CREDITS 172

INDEX 173

FOREWORD

CHARLESTON'S COLUMNED PORCHES

The most distinctive feature of Charleston, represented in almost every block of the city, is a dwelling called the Single House, one of the few house plans that is probably of purely American origin. Because it evolved from row houses with businesses on their ground floors and dwellings above, it appears in commercial as well as residential areas. Because its simple plan worked well on a large as well as a small scale, it characterizes both rich neighborhoods and poor. Charleston has nearly three thousand Single Houses.

Another distinctive feature of Charleston is the large number of other building types that have been in continuous use since they were built. Other house types, such as the Double House or the twin-parlor house, are not unique to Charleston, but they are well represented and have been given the appearance of Charleston houses through the addition of piazzas, the columned porches that run along the side and across the back of most of the city's early houses. In addition there are numerous early churches, public buildings, fraternal halls, warehouses, and commercial buildings. The survival of these buildings and neighborhoods makes Charleston exceptional as a historic city.

These buildings have usually survived because they were well designed and well built in the first place and so were worth keeping. Nonetheless many of them would undoubtedly have been destroyed in the years between the Civil War and World War II, if Charleston had not been so poor. Hardship forced Charlestonians to recognize what most American cities have only begun to appreciate, that a good building is not easily replaced.

A particularly enjoyable aspect of Charleston is that the settings of many of its buildings have also survived. The waterfront is still largely open, and many streets are lined with trees; in addition there are hundreds of fine gardens. Walking along Charleston's tree-lined streets is still the best way to see and to enjoy the city, to be able to stop and examine the unusually fine craftsmanship of its ironwork, the handsomely carved woodwork surrounding doorways, and many other details that cannot be seen elsewhere in such variety.

This book tells a great deal about Charleston by considering five significant houses in detail. Shirley Abbott describes these buildings and their occupants and furnishings, pointing out what is typical and extraordinary about Charleston. The accompanying photographs show how enjoyable a walk through the city can be.

GENE WADDELL
CHARLESTON, SOUTH CAROLINA

INTRODUCTION

Charleston is and always will be a small town, the citadel of a "hereditary Nobility," as its founders willed it to be. In its early days Charleston was a walled city and in some sense has continued as such, though the walls long ago vanished. The boundary markers of historic Charleston today are, in addition to its implacable sense of self, the Ashley and the Cooper rivers, which meet at the tip of the Charleston peninsula, and Broad Street, the third side of the triangle. Within this district, along the streets with their ancient names (such as Meeting, Tradd, Church, King, Legare) stand a high proportion of the important houses of Charleston—important because they are unique and beautiful, a national heritage. Many of them are older than the United States itself.

The narrow sidewalk, the closed shutters, the ironwork, the white walls alternating with an occasional pink are elements in the charm of a Charleston street.

The best way to begin seeing the houses of Charleston is the simplest. Drive from the airport or the interstate down the peninsula to the very heart of things. Compared with the outskirts of most cities, the northern reaches of Charleston are orderly and presentable. You pass the hamburger stands and motels that you might expect, the drop-in daycare centers, gas

The symmetry and rectangularity of the facade, as well as its stately portico that harks back to Greco-Roman grandeur, mark this house as a fine example of Georgian design. Built about 1769 by a wealthy slave merchant, Miles Brewton, it is one of Charleston's, and America's, architectural treasures.

stations, garages, and right-to-life billboards, all of which you might also encounter driving into Des Moines, Iowa; but here the drab artifacts of daily life are more than compensated for by the vivid sky, the small, neatly laced-up palmetto trees, the oleanders, and the tall crepe myrtles. Whatever the season, something is nearly always in flower, pink or white blossoms against the rich, variegated greens.

The distance downtown is short, and quite soon you run out of freeway and find yourself ejected into a seedy neighborhood on Meeting Street, the main thoroughfare, which runs north and south and probably derives its name from the meeting house, or church, farther on down. You pass the Charleston Museum, full of lovely things as it happens, and the oldest museum in America, now housed in a windowless brick pile with all the architectural charm of a munitions dump. You catch a glimpse, farther south, of the Confederate Museum (do they never forget? no, never) in a more seemly old Charleston building, and then as Meeting crosses Broad all at once you find yourself in another world. Like Dorothy when the tornado deposits her in the Land of Oz, you may not know exactly where you have landed, but clearly this is not Kansas.

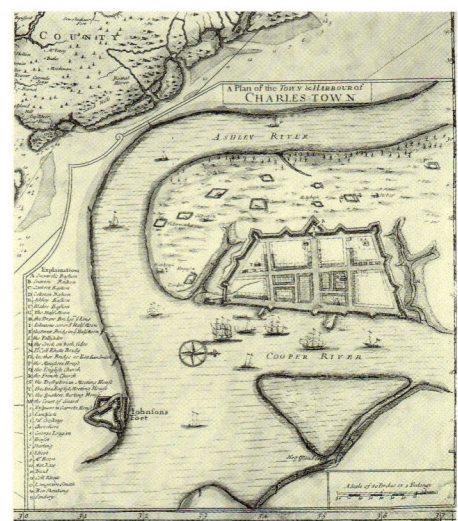

Drawn about 1704 when the settlement was thirty-odd years old, this map shows the confluence of the Ashley and the Cooper and a walled town with a few houses outside.

You are in a district so well kept, so freshly painted, so unequivocably of another century as to make you feel an intruder in a private domain. A number of public buildings catch your eye: St. Michael's Episcopal Church, with its Roman portico, its immaculate white steeple, and its air of authority both temporal and spiritual; the post office; city hall; the county courthouse; and farther down another church with a neoclassical portico, this one for the Presbyterians. But what define the cityscape as you proceed down Meeting Street are the houses, two or three stories tall, set so close to the sidewalks that you could put your hand through the windows, set so close to one another that they might be row houses with common walls. Then you see that, in fact, they stand apart from one another, separated by long, narrow gardens shut off at the street end by wrought-iron gates.

The doors to these houses, fitted out with highly polished brass and flush with the street, you might imagine would lead to the entrance hall or even the parlor. But as you walk past, you notice that many of these doors are not what they seem. If you

INTRODUCTION

knocked at one of them and were admitted, you would find yourself not inside the house but on the side porch (the piazza, as they call it here, with soft *z*'s and no hint of the Italianate *t*). You would go from the outside to another kind of outside. For the newcomer to Charleston admitted to what he expects to be the inner sanctum, this is a pleasant shock, a kind of flirtatious, beguiling trait for a house to possess. And it is a trait peculiar to the houses of this city.

The streets, though a few are still paved with Colonial cobblestones, are as pristine as the paint job on St. Michael's Church. Except for the occasional eighteenth-century carriage mount, or boot scraper, or hitching post, ordinary street furniture is curiously absent. There are, thank heaven, a few discreet fire hydrants, painted in agreeable colors. You will search in vain, however, for the pay phones, newsstands, coffee shops, and souvenir stands that both humanize and disfigure most cities, particularly those that live by the tourist trade. You cannot help sensing the presence of a heavy female hand here. The ladies of the various preservation committees have completed their civilizing mission. Though Charleston is still a city with traffic in the streets and real people living in the houses, the district south of Broad is a kind of outdoor drawing room, carefully controlled. The tidiness is all part of the charm, however, and may be taken as the essential quality of modern Charleston, if any such thing as "modern" Charleston exists.

Already a venerable old American city in 1831, Charleston had many mansions. The houses on East Battery, above, with a view of the harbor, owed their existence to a new seawall. Then, as now, this was a fashionable and pleasant place to promenade.

The city did not begin her life as a museum of tea tables and mantelpieces. Rather, she started out as a frenetic, dangerous, dirty seventeenth-century seaport, an English toehold in the new land. Charleston was settled in 1670 on a charter from Charles II of England, the "merry monarch" and father of his people, or at least, as the joke went, of a great many of them. He gave his mandate for the new colony to eight grandees of his court: the earls of Craven and of Clarendon, the duke of Albemarle, Sir George Carteret, Sir John Colleton, Lord John Berkeley, his brother William, and Lord Anthony Ashley Cooper, later earl of Shaftesbury. Though their patronymics are strewn around the Carolina landscape, none of these "lords proprietors" ever set foot in Charleston. But nevertheless, their wishes shaped it. The

INTRODUCTION

lords proprietors wanted a city (in fact wanted many cities), planned in advance, laid out according to a checkerboard plan. Charleston was a city from its birth, not some fort or trading post that grew randomly into a town. Their lordships reasoned that a city can protect itself against invaders; it also provides a place for businessmen to congregate and deal with one another. And, moreover, the first Charlestonians, laying out their neat streets and setting their houses on small lots, must have felt that civilized men needed to be close, that they needed neighbors and noise in the streets, needed to observe and be observed, needed the bustle of society.

Charleston's economic base lay in the plantations of the Low Country. Drayton Hall, nine miles away, was built in the late 1730s—one of the finest of all manors in South Carolina.

The city plan had underpinnings, for the proprietors had thought of the economy as well. Lord Ashley commissioned his secretary, the philosopher John Locke, to draw up a constitution for the colony. It offered religious freedom and a clean shot at getting rich quick, both powerful attractions for the better sort of colonist. The powers of the slaveholder over his chattels he defined as absolute. The rent on an acre of land was only a penny's worth of silver; a holding of twelve thousand acres created the owner a baron, twenty-four thousand acres made him a "cassique," and forty-eight thousand a landgrave. The headright system also played a part in acquisition of land. According to the number of "heads," or slaves, he owned, a man was entitled to land: in the early days, 150 acres for himself and 150 for each manservant. Since news of this sort travels fast, the English who came both from England and from the English colonies in Barbados, St. Kitts, and Bermuda were joined by French Huguenots (Protestants)—fleeing religious persecution by their kings and queens—by the Dutch, by contingents of Sephardic Jews from Holland, and by the Scots.

In their taste and manners, the early Charlestonians were European, but in their eye for the main chance and their eagerness to display their newly minted wealth in the form of domestic architecture, they were indeed Americans. They built the first American boomtown and managed to keep it going for considerably longer than most boomtowns ever endure. Though the lineal descendants of these first families still revere their forefathers as aristocrats and blue bloods, the old gentlemen were fortunately not too high-minded to make a quick deal or handle a bill of lading.

INTRODUCTION

In Charleston in the early days, refreshingly enough, nobility came not from blood but from wits or money. Like everything else, it was for sale.

By the mid-eighteenth century, the South Carolina planters were among the richest men in the colonies, outclassed by only a few tobacco planters in Virginia and millionaires in New York. Unlike the Virginians, however, they had created a city, which must have looked (and smelled and sounded) much like a miniature London. Horse-drawn wagons, drays, and carriages toiled up and down the streets, vendors shouted, and slaves were sold at the block. Executions and lesser punishments, such as whipping, took place in public, and the casual visitor could pass his mornings watching a pirate be hanged or a criminal branded. Or, failing to find justice being meted out, he might have counted the masts in port and the barrels of rice on the wharves. This was a city where men came to make their fortunes and enjoy the fruits thereof. They were housebuilders by their very nature. They wanted lovely houses, staffed with servants to see to the needs of ladies and gentlemen, very different houses from the gaunt and godly timber-frame dwellings of Puritan Salem. Although the planters were of course at liberty to build the finest country manors they could afford, the plantations served the city, and every planter maintained a town house. Not one house from the early days survives, but Charlestonians have historically brought a special genius to the building of their houses. Surely even in the seventeenth century they were honing their skills.

In this watercolor of 1800, black men and women on a plantation near Charleston sing and dance to the music of African instruments: the molo *(a banjo prototype) and drums. Rice and indigo were the major crops, and slavery made them feasible.*

Since a house proclaims what relationships the owner intends to have with his neighbors, building a house is always a political act. Perhaps the clearest expression of the American democratic ideal is the house in the middle of a small plot of land, with a front porch where the family sits, as if on a stage, in full view of the world and full hearing of whatever commotion arises in the houses next door and across the street. But an expression of quite another political ideal is the quintessential Charleston house, the Single House, which is one room wide and three deep, with its narrow end toward the street and usually (but not always) with a one- or two-story piazza on the side. It is almost a row house, sitting a few scant feet from its neighbors but turning a blank

11

INTRODUCTION

wall toward them, a house separated from the street by only a wall; yet by means of its piazza door it finds a way both to give and to deny access, since the door leads not to the parlor but to the porch. This house is part of public life but hides from it, with its family "stage" hidden behind a door and behind a lacy, locked iron gate, and its functional parts (the kitchen, the outhouse, the storehouses, and the servants' quarters) compactly concealed in the walled courtyard out back. In one sense it is a democratic house plan because a Single House can be poor or grand, depending on its owner's fortune, and thus it cuts across class lines. In another sense it is incurably elitist, showing as little of itself to the world as possible and sequestering its inmates as though in a harem.

The Single House, Charleston's distinctive contribution to American architecture, did not evolve all at once. Of the Single Houses now standing, only two hundred were built before the Revolutionary War, and none in the seventeenth century. (A view of the city drawn in 1739 shows no Single Houses at all.) By no means are all the fine houses of Charleston Single Houses. Some of the most famous are Double Houses—that is, a nearly square house with a room in each corner and a central hall, or sidehall or twin-parlor houses with grand staircases visible from the front door, or built according to some other plan. Yet there are features common to almost all the notable Charleston dwellings. They are all city houses, affording quick access to public places—the churches, the wharves, the markets—of the town, and they are marked with all kinds of adaptations to city life. The windowless wall, for example, so typical for one side of the Single House, was probably a safety measure. In the eighteenth and nineteenth centuries, Charleston was regularly devastated by fires, and if the house next door happens to be ablaze, a wall with no windows, or in some cases only one small one, is much less likely to catch fire.

Emblems such as this indicated that the houses they embellished carried fire insurance. Fires were commonplace in Charleston, sometimes destroying hundreds of homes at a time.

Furthermore, in spite of their present-day elegance, many of the houses of Charleston were built not only as homes but also as places of business. The downstairs parlor was as often as not a reception room where the master of the house spent his mornings with other tradesmen or sea captains or commercial acquaintances, planning future enterprises or counting up profits and losses. For this

INTRODUCTION

Hurricanes and earthquakes also battered the city's architecture. This iron cross, a memento of calamity, is an earthquake bolt, securing one end of a long rod that runs through the house to strengthen and brace it after earthquake damage.

reason the family living quarters and the company rooms—the dining rooms and drawing rooms—are most often on the second floor. This made sense not only because the first floor might be full of traffic but also because the upstairs windows, open wide, would more easily catch the sea breeze.

The crushingly humid, subtropical climate of the Carolina Low Country has influenced taste in other ways as well. For one thing it undoubtedly led to the almost universal acceptance of the piazza by Charleston builders. The word comes not, as one might expect, directly from Italy but, like so much else in Charleston, directly from England. In 1750 Samuel Johnson defined a piazza as "a walk under a roof supported by pillars." A century earlier the great architect Inigo Jones had built a "piazza," or covered walkway, at Covent Garden in London. The word meant "square," but the English applied it to the walkway and gave it their own pronunciation. In Charleston the piazza, whether it had one or two tiers, provided some shade for that side of the house, as well as a secluded and no doubt highly entertaining view of Charleston street life. It also—and surely this was part of its appeal—gave the builder a chance to add some columns and capitals and fancy woodwork to the exterior of his house. The piazza, whether on the front or the side of the house, is to most observers an enchanting feature—breezy and romantic, however functional and sensible it may be.

Sitting out of doors was hardly the chief activity of a Charleston family. A house begets work, and must have workers to do it. From the days of its founding, Carolina based its economy on the slave trade and its well-being on slave labor. Charlestonians made large fortunes on the trans-Atlantic slave trade and on the domestic trade as well. Slaves worked the plantations, and they serviced the town houses; the slave population of Charleston was always highly visible. For every white man, woman, and child living in the elegant town houses, there might have been several blacks. One authority estimates that a wealthy Carolina family in Colonial times might have been outnumbered ten to one by its servants, at least in the country; in town the ratio was probably two to one. Even existing in a condition of servitude, no population this large can be without its influence. A man building a house for his family and a contingent of servants builds a different house than for his family alone. In addition servants in bondage had to be contained. They could not be allowed too much freedom; their owners needed to know where they were. This may account in part for the walled gardens of Charleston, the proximity of the houses, the discreetly locked gates.

The Pringle House, built in 1774, is a classic Single House, one room wide. Its long piazza (above) is behind a front door opening directly into the street.

But surely, too, so large a work force contributed substantially to the well-being of the city. The tour guides in the museum houses these days occasionally tell their audience that the woodwork or the plastered ceilings or the handsomely carved banisters or the furnishings were created by slave artisans. "Up to ninety percent of what you see is the creation of black hands," one tour guide recently proclaimed—a theory without any factual basis whatever. Certainly Charleston had its slave carpenters and carvers and smiths, but they occupied the lowest rungs of artisanship. While some slaves became highly skilled as cabinetmakers, their white masters kept them in their places as laborers and apprentices and seldom gave them the chance to design anything. Skilled whites were anxious never to have to compete with skilled slaves. City ordinances, moreover, controlled the number of slave apprentices a craftsman might employ.

Yet one way the slaves undeniably served the purposes of domestic architecture in Charleston was that, in the large sense, their hard labor on the Low Country plantations created the wealth that built the houses. And, in a more immediate sense, their labor within the houses made possible the exquisite rooms and furnishings, for such things require endless maintenance. Houses filled with brass and silver and fine china, with wood floors ever in need of scrubbing or painting, with linens that must be painstakingly washed and ironed, with crystal chandeliers in need of dismantling and washing every few months to enliven their sparkle, with finely painted surfaces that must occasionally be sanded and refinished (to name only a few of the tasks that had to be performed) would be uninhabitable without skillful, patient servants, whether the servants are slave or free.

The houses of Charleston, however, speak of other matters than social and

INTRODUCTION

economic necessity, for, in the end, a house is more than an adaptation to basic needs. Generally speaking most of the finest houses of Charleston were built within a span of fifty or sixty years beginning about 1760. So far as is known, not one of them was designed by a professional architect in our sense of the word; but they are of a piece, with several qualities in common—dignity, proportion, restraint. The eighteenth-century houses of Charleston, in particular, express a unified sensibility, are one of the most lyrical expressions of that sensibility in America.

The terms that architectural historians use to describe this sensibility, or style, vary. The visitor to Charleston will hear a great deal about the Georgian and the Adamesque styles, which sometimes appear to be synonymous and sometimes mutually exclusive, depending on who uses them. "Georgian" architecture takes its name from the first three Hanoverian kings of England, Georges I, II, and III, during whose reigns (beginning in 1714) the English neoclassical style flourished in England as well as in the colonies. This was an age of grandeur that found its inspiration in the formalism of Renaissance architecture, an age that demanded noble Greco-Roman ornamentation on its facades and classical allusions in its poems. This same spirit expressed itself—on a smaller scale—in a variety of American houses. The Miles Brewton house has one of the finest Georgian facades in Charleston, or America. Its most noticeable characteristics are the handsome brickwork; the double-tiered porticoes and the pediment (borrowed from the Greco-Roman world and used as a noble addendum to the building rather than as its controlling form); and most of all the proportion, the balanced placement of the windows, the doorways on both upper and lower porches—the main door with its fanlight and pilasters, the upper one understated and plain. But what makes it so characteristically Georgian is neither the brickwork nor the proportions but the squarishness, the overall impression of solidity and predictability.

The asymmetrical plan of the George Eveleigh house, above, on Church Street was very common in Charleston in the first half of the eighteenth century. The house has a two-story piazza, and its first owner, a fur trader, built it about 1743.

Adamesque is a further development of Georgian, taking its name from the Scottish architect Robert Adam, one of the most successful designers and decorators of the late eighteenth century—or any period. His style is lighter than the Georgian, more attenuated, more brittle. A devoted classicist, Robert Adam was also a worshiper of Roman architecture. But what he admired most in his beloved "Ancients" was their decorative bent. Roman interiors, he once observed, were "all delicacy, gaiety, grace, and beauty." An example of the Adamesque style in Charleston is the Nathaniel Russell house (Chapter Three), also in brick, with its polygonal bay on the garden side, its wrought-iron balconies, and, in particular, its famous "flying" staircase, all curvature and grace and daring.

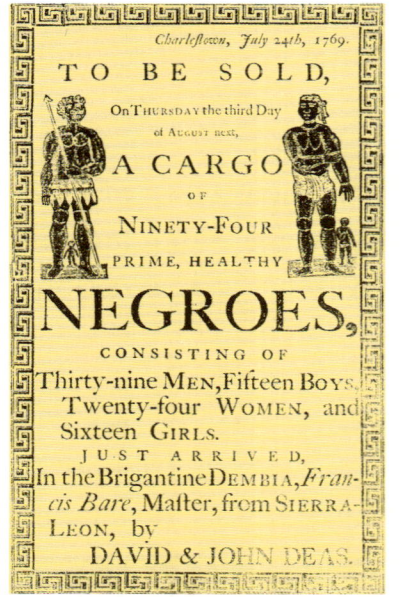

Datelined "Charleston, July 24, 1769," this broadside is a glimpse of one side of the city's thriving commercial life—the slave trade, which made many fortunes.

Whatever name they go by, the Georgian and the Adamesque styles arise from a deep belief in order. This is the counterpart in domestic architecture of Newton's perfectly tuned universe. Its every line expresses optimism, balance, the sense of proportion, and a self-conscious connection with a rational past. Look again, for example, at the facade of the Miles Brewton house. Here, in an outpost of empire in 1769, a millionaire merchant built a house whose classical portico proclaims its descent from the great Italian villas of the Renaissance, as well as the public buildings of Greece and Rome. Yet, at the same time, it is perfectly English and in its restraint and elegance pays homage to the English gentleman's code. This two-story brick facade, symmetrical in every detail, is forthright and masculine. Enclosed by its elaborate wrought-iron fence, it is a domain to itself, and a closely contained one.

No society capable of building such houses as these could long be satisfied to take its orders from a bureaucracy overseas. In the battle for American independence, South Carolina sacrificed more men than any other colony, and Charleston endured bitter years of British occupation. General Sir Henry Clinton, commander of the invading forces, took the Miles Brewton house as headquarters, no doubt because it was the most comfortable in town, but perhaps also in hope of stamping out the pride it so plainly expressed.

Like other great houses of America, the houses of Charleston stood for something—a web of values and beliefs, uncounted hours of care and labor, a culture with an impossibly high melting point. Catastrophes of every kind hit this small city. Fires, particularly in Colonial times, would swallow up half the buildings in one gulp; and one of the worst conflagrations occurred in 1861 while the city was at war with the United States. Earthquakes have come with terrible regularity, the worst perhaps in 1812 and 1886; and hurricanes and floods have not spared Charleston either. But after the fires the city always rebuilt; and after the earthquakes the citizenry patched their houses and pulled the frames together with giant bolts, whose blunt ends ornament many a side wall and facade today. After the hurricanes people mopped up the mud and repaired the damage and went on. Perhaps the worst disaster from the psychological as well as the material point of view was the Civil War, during which the city was besieged by Federal troops and battered with heavy artillery. Fortunately, however, General Sherman did not have time to come and raze Charleston, and thus the city was spared the devastation wrought on the South Carolina capital at Columbia and on Richmond. The damage inflicted in those years was slow to be repaired. But Charleston remained.

This oil painting by Charleston artist Christian Mayr portrays the officers of the volunteer fire department in 1841. This was the period when Charleston acquired its first fire-fighting equipment, which was manned partly by slaves as well as white volunteers.

No visitor admiring the fragile-looking little houses today—the lacy balustrades, the tea tables, and the drawing rooms of Charleston—should forget that some part of the city's soul is made of steel. Though its thoroughfares may be as exquisite as its architecture, Charleston retains its primeval toughness. "The civil defense people talk of a plan for evacuating Charleston, in case of nuclear attack," a lady of Tradd Street observed recently. "But I wouldn't have any *idea* of leaving Charleston. The hurricanes and earthquakes and the British and even the Northern invaders couldn't put an end to us, and neither will any atom bomb." One hopes that she is right.

1
HEYWARD-WASHINGTON HOUSE
HOME OF THE BRAVE

Charleston has many houses that express the ideals of the eighteenth-century gentleman—his love of a leisurely and methodical life, his expectation of being well served at home and of having the means to offer hospitality to all callers—and none expresses these ideals more succinctly than the Heyward-Washington house at 87 Church Street. Its every line speaks of respectability and good sense and marks it as the sort of dwelling a successful lawyer, perhaps, would want for his family. Thomas Heyward, the first resident and owner, was indeed a lawyer, as well as a planter, patriot, soldier, and later a judge. He was also a revolutionary, being among the South Carolina delegates who sat in the Continental Congress and signed the Declaration of Independence. However high-minded the principle, this was a treasonous act for which the perpetrators risked imprisonment and death.

Thomas Heyward appears as a decisive young man in this copy by Charles Fraser of an oil by Jeremiah Theus, one of the most sought-after "limners" in the city.

Yet this scarcely looks like the home of a radical. The brick exterior is a model of plain, solid workmanship, lacking any neoclassical flourishes or even the amenity of a side porch. The house is five windows wide, with the front door set right in the middle, just as a child might draw it. The building fills nearly the whole width of the lot, the northern wall being attached to the house next door, and the south corner

This pre-Revolutionary town house has sheltered more than one rebellious American. Thomas Heyward and his wife defied the British from within this house, and later Sarah Grimké, an abolitionist and feminist, lived here. Here, too, George Washington was undeniably a houseguest.

having a narrow gate leading to the garden.

To any lover of urban architecture, and of houses designed to sit cheek-by-jowl with their neighbors, this three-story building is a classic of the genre. Its counterparts still stand in London, Philadelphia, Washington, New York, and Boston—serviceable city houses with doors and windows that open directly onto the life of the street. Though conversations on Church Street these days tend to be conducted in a tasteful whisper, the daily round in the eighteenth century was a good deal livelier. Like every Charleston thoroughfare, this was a merchant's and trader's street. Across the way from 87 Church was a bookbinder's and stationer's shop, and up the street the assembly hall, where bidders at auction could buy anything from imported wines to human beings. A general housewares store was only a few doors away, as well as a milliner and a baker. There were other houses, too, from which children, servants, and dogs emerged whenever they had the chance. Carriages, horses, and wagons came and went. This is exactly the sort of town house a political man would love, the sort of neighborhood he would thrive in when he left the comparative isolation of his country estate.

Above the dining room's Georgian-style mantel hangs a portrait of Daniel Heyward, a copy of one by Theus, who often portrayed Charleston's gentry. The side chairs are Chippendale in style.

The house also met the needs of a man with an active social life. Off the central hall with its mahogany stairs are four rooms, all of which are likely to have served public purposes. The rooms are only moderate in size, the proportions homey and circumspect. The dark woodwork, the stolid look of the entry hall mark the house as

---

Opposite: Circumspect in dimension and decor, the dining room exemplifies the taste of late Colonial America. One extravagant touch is the mirror with its heavy Chinese Chippendale frame. The table is set here for the mid-afternoon dinner, which would have been carried into the house from the backyard kitchen.

Overleaf: This is one of America's finest Colonial drawing rooms, filled as it is with Charleston-made furnishings in the Chippendale style and boasting a mantelpiece and other woodwork probably carved by the great local cabinetmaker Thomas Elfe. The oval looking glass, with rococo carvings, is of the period.

Georgian: no Adamesque exuberance here. Upstairs, nevertheless, is one of Charleston's most beautiful drawing rooms, spacious and wide, with woodwork intricately wrought by some master craftsman, perhaps the greatest Charleston craftsman of all, Thomas Elfe. The furnishings in the room today, eighteenth-century treasures belonging to the Charleston Museum, are of the style that Thomas Heyward would have purchased for his drawing room. It was surely a source of pride for him that a room of such dignity and elegance could have been designed by the craftsmen of his own city. Here indeed was a fit place for a patriot to play host.

The house was commissioned in 1772, either by Thomas Heyward or his father, Daniel, looking after his son's interests. Like many promising young Charlestonians of that era, Thomas had got his education in London, reading law at the Middle Temple. Thomas wrote his father from London that he was spending much of his time at the theater, adding, "I think the stage affords a fine scene for improvement as well as pleasure, especially to one who is intended for what I am. It is a very proper school to learn a good delivery with a graceful action." Returning to Charleston in 1770 to begin his career, Thomas acquired the Church Street property as well as more than a thousand acres of farmland. In 1773 he married Elizabeth Matthewes, sister of one of his compatriots at law school. The new mansion on Church Street was finished by then, and the young couple moved into it.

By the time he married, Thomas was already a public figure in Charleston, a lawyer with a growing reputation, a pillar of St. Michael's Church, a lieutenant in the Charleston artillery, even a curator of the Charleston Museum, founded in 1773 to promote interest in science. He was also an active believer in American independence. Few men in his position were happy with the demeaning status of "Colonial," or with being subject to the whim of functionaries and to whatever fiscal indignities London saw fit to impose. While he had been a student, Heyward had spent some time in the grandest of all London theaters, Parliament, and had concluded that the men in power there were "desirous of sowing the seeds of discord between the mother-country and her colonies and making the Americans the most abject slaves."

And thus in 1776 he was a natural choice to go to the Continental Congress and to

A corner of the overmantel, here in detail, shows the elegance of the wood carving. The mahogany fretwork is Thomas Elfe's characteristic pattern, which he either designed himself or learned from another carver. In his account book he notes that ten pounds was his charge for chimneypiece frets.

sign Thomas Jefferson's Declaration of Independence. When the time came to fight, he did so as a captain in the Charleston artillery and was wounded in action. In 1780, after Lord Cornwallis took Charleston, he arrested Heyward and several of his friends and eventually transported them to Saint Augustine, Florida. He clapped them not in some grim dungeon but a pleasant stone house with "a large orange garden," which the young men rented from a local clergyman. Thomas kept everybody's spirits up by composing and singing patriotic songs.

Back home at Church Street, Elizabeth Heyward was doing her best for the war effort. She had living with her a sister and several nephews and nieces. The Heywards themselves had a six-year-old boy, one of four children born in the seven years of their marriage and the only one who lived. In May 1781 the British ordered all the householders of Charleston to light candles in their windows as a gesture of gratitude for a year of British occupation. Elizabeth obstinately kept her house dark. A mob assembled and threw trash at her windows, and the forces of occupation threatened to tear the house down. The visitor to the house can get an idea of her courage by looking out the drawing room windows on the second story, so close to the street, so vulnerable to any flying rock. She never gave in, even though her sister was ill and died in the aftermath of the commotion.

St. Michael's Church, at Meeting and Broad, was Thomas Heyward's church. Very little changed over the years, it has always been a Charleston landmark.

A few months later, thanks to an exchange of war prisoners, Thomas arrived in Philadelphia, where Elizabeth and their son soon joined him. That fall they had the satisfaction of knowing that Cornwallis had surrendered to General Washington at Yorktown. The next May, still in Philadelphia, Elizabeth won the "prize of beauty" at a large party given by General Washington. But in August she was dead, having just given birth to a new son, who outlived her for only a short time. Childbirth in the eighteenth century was considerably more hazardous than defying an armed mob. One of the underlying themes in the story of Charleston or any other city of the time

This fragile French spinet with a decorated lid is late seventeenth century and very rare. It is an example of the kind of musical instrument the American colonists imported after they acquired the drawing rooms for them, and their wives and daughters had the leisure time to play them.

is the death of young wives and mothers. By the time Elizabeth died, Thomas's father was married to his third young wife (he had had one Mary and two Elizabeths), and Thomas himself remarried after the usual interval—another Elizabeth, age seventeen.

After the death of his wife and baby, Thomas Heyward went back to Charleston, where he became a judge. By the end of the 1780s, he began to spend less time in town and more on his plantation. And thus, because he was not in it, his Church Street house had its moment of fame when George Washington, now president, indisputably slept under its roof for a whole week in April 1791, thus giving the house the second part of its name. At the peak of his popularity, the president decided to tour his southern dominions, and no king could have been welcomed with greater pomp and joy. At this moment, as at no time since, Charleston felt solidly a part of the American endeavor, and Washington was one of their own. Balls, breakfasts, and receptions were planned, and all the poets of Charleston set to work composing suitable odes, as in the following example: "Prudence and courage form my hero's mind,/ to every change of fate alike resign'd;/ The virtues which illume his daring soul/ Have spread his fame from Indus to the pole."

The hero's policy was not to impose on private citizens, but luckily Judge Heyward was in the country, and the housing committee rented his mansion as presidential lodgings. All Charleston turned out to meet the president: he was rowed across the Cooper River in a twelve-oared barge, saluted with cannon, greeted by a flotilla. A grand procession took him to Heyward's house, and the president noted with satisfaction in his diary, "The lodgings provided for me in this place were very good, being the furnished house of a Gentleman at present in the Country; but occupied by a person placed there on purpose to accommodate me & who was paid in the same manner as any other letter of lodgings would have been paid." Charlestonians still remember with pleasure the opinions of Washington on the local women (elegantly dressed, all of them handsome) and on the people in general ("wealthy—Gay—& hospitable").

Thomas Heyward and George Washington play the leading roles in the tales the tour guides spin about 87 Church Street, but like other houses this one offers its

In the bedroom upstairs is the bed, attributed to Thomas Elfe, that Thomas Heyward slept in. It has finely turned mahogany posts and poplar rails and a headboard that could be removed when the bed was pushed to the middle of the room in summer. On the opposite wall is a Charleston-made clothespress.

interplay of identities, some of them antagonistic and hidden from view. Preoccupied with his rice plantation, Thomas Heyward resigned his judgeship and sold the house in 1794 to John Grimké, who had studied law in London with him. Like every Charleston surname, Grimké is an old one, and French as well. John Grimké and his wife were every inch aristocrats, and marvelously prolific besides. When they moved into the house, they already had six children and eventually produced eight more. With two adults, children of all sizes, and perhaps a dozen slaves, the house was an endless bustle — footsteps always on the stair and no privacy for anyone, even with the children sequestered on the third story. The servants of course lived in the garden outbuildings, doing much of their work in the enormous kitchen and wash kitchen that opened into the garden and sleeping on the floor above. With no plumbing and few baths (the water supply came from a cistern), and the "necessary" in the garden close to the kitchen, the noises and the smells must have been overpowering, though no more so than in any house.

But for one of the Grimké daughters, however, the house turned into an unbearable prison. Her name was Sarah, and she had been only a baby when her parents moved to Church Street. She should by all rights have grown up like any other young girl, learning the ladylike arts, entering society, making a suitable marriage. But as she later wrote, "I, however, always had one terrible drawback. Slavery was a millstone around my neck and marred my comfort from the time I can remember myself." Until her sister Angelina was born, Sarah was alone in her outlook; but Angelina, too, as she grew up, was equally unnerved by the spectacle of suffering and injustice all around her. What to the rest of the world seemed perfectly ordinary sickened these two children. Sarah recorded that in one of the best families in Charleston, she had seen agonizing punishments inflicted upon slaves. One woman related that "she had had the ears of her waiting maid slit for some petty theft. This she told me in the presence of the girl...." One institution in Charleston at the time was the so-called workhouse, where slaves were sent to be punished by professionals. On one errand or another, the two young girls often walked past this building and heard the cries from inside the walls.

The Grimké sisters stood little chance of taking their place as proper Charleston

Southern householders very often installed their kitchens in outbuildings. This saved the main house from excessive heat as well as the threat of fire. The kitchen building here has survived in almost its original state. Behind the main hearth was the washroom; the servants slept on the second floor.

matrons, and both eventually left their native state, moving north to play an active part in the abolitionist movement and to become the founding mothers of American feminism. "Women," wrote Sarah, "ought to feel a peculiar sympathy in the colored man's wrong, for, like him, she has been accused of mental inferiority...." During the 1840s the Charleston police were on notice to arrest either of the Grimké sisters on sight, should they ever return home. Wisely, perhaps, they settled in New Jersey, Angelina having married Theodore Weld, a leader of the abolitionists. The sisters never returned to Charleston, did not see their city conquered. But they did see an end to slavery and knew they had played a role in ending it.

The mansion on Church Street had passed out of the Grimkés' hands long before the two sisters fled north, and it was never again to see great days. It became, successively, a boarding house and a bakery. When a twentieth-century collector of Americana threatened to buy the drawing room, dismantle it, and cart it off to another city, the Charleston Museum (and other persons and organizations) bought the home of Thomas Heyward—their early curator—and set it to rights again.

The garden of this house is particularly pleasant, with basil, bay, rosemary, and other herbs burgeoning outside the kitchen door. Anyone who has ever cooked on an open hearth can imagine the intensity of the fire on a spring day and the fragrance of a Charleston dinner—the bread baking, fish frying, rice steaming in a kettle, and perhaps a basket of oysters on the kitchen table waiting to be shucked. Because the outbuildings have survived in something like their original state, the presence of the generations of servants is almost palpable here, where they cooked so many meals. Somehow, too, the Grimké sisters have left their mark on the house, defying the social order as they did, just as Elizabeth and Thomas Heyward had defied the British. This dwelling of patriots and rebels, exemplary in its design, reflects not only the gentlemanly ideal but many of the complexities, even tragedies, of Charleston life.

Opposite: On the plain, serviceable pine dough box sits a variety of crockery and other utensils. Above it, on the kitchen wall, hang a round griddle, a metal broiling rack, a wooden pipe box, and a sheaf of dried herbs.

Overleaf: Hanging from the cranes and hooks inside the massive fireplace, kettles of soup would have simmered, while roasts turned on a spit and pies or cornbread cooked in three-legged pots in the hot ashes. The beehive oven on the right, which required great skill to heat to the proper level, was for baking breads, puddings, and custards. The broad table provided a work surface. In the foreground, in front of an armchair, is a churn.

GRAND ENTRANCES

A visitor strolling through the oldest part of Charleston, south of Broad Street, will find remarkable doors and gates at every turning. In the eighteenth and early nineteenth centuries, impressive entrances were a mark of status, and builders lavished considerable care on their design. When they wanted to suggest long-standing wealth and power, they turned to European models, especially Georgian England. One of the borrowings most in evidence is the fanlight, a semicircular window above a door. In its usual form the window's triangular panes radiate upward, but many ingenious variations were possible, for example the inverted fanlight at Blacklock House (page 43), whose cascading curves suggest the petals of a flower. To dramatize entrances to courtyards and gardens, as well as to ensure privacy, builders designed spectacular gates made of wrought iron. Some of Charleston's fine ironwork from the Colonial period was lost in 1886, when an earthquake struck, but enough examples survived to offer models for later artisans. By the middle of the nineteenth century, cast iron began to appear in combination with handwrought work. Casting the iron in molds saved time and allowed finer surface detail without necessarily sacrificing originality—molds were often created for one house and then destroyed. Throughout the old city Charleston's doorways and gateways offer glimpses into piazzas and gardens, managing both to protect and display, hide and reveal.

The Victorian door at 1 East Battery embodies a reserved elegance appropriate to a great antebellum house.

The harmonious and understated design for 14 Legare has a fanlight, pilasters, and crescent-shaped steps.

This etched glass door in a decorative setting is original to the house at 26 Battery, built in the 1850s.

The neoclassical entrance at 54 Meeting Street is fairly typical of Charleston doors that open out onto piazzas. The columns

flanking the doorway are original and date from about 1800.

At top are the carved wood brackets on the sandstone columns of the Dock Street Theater. Directly above is the unique fluted fanlight at the Nathaniel Russell house (Chapter Three).

At top is the inverted fanlight at Blacklock House, located at 18 Bull Street. Directly above is a more typical fanlight, which is over the door at the Villa Margherita.

The lacy wrought-iron gate at 8 Legare Street makes use of the lyre pattern borrowed from classical design.

Made in the 1930s the gate at the Dock Street Theater is hand wrought—modern design at its best.

Like much of the ironwork in Charleston, the fence at 116 Broad Street combines cast and wrought iron with no sacrifice to

the elegance of the design. Here the vertical bars are wrought, the central urns cast in molds.

The wrought-iron gate at Miles Brewton House is made more imposing by the spiky chevaux de frise. *Named for a fortification devised in Friesland, in the Netherlands, to defend against attackers on horseback, this device*

was adopted by some homeowners to discourage intruders. According to legend this one was added to the original gate after a slave insurrection that occurred in 1822.

2
MANIGAULT HOUSE
A CHARLESTON DYNASTY

"It is better to overlook than to avenge" is the motto of the family that built the mansion at 350 Meeting Street—an expression of magnanimity and tolerance that the house itself reflects. Its generous proportions and wide entrance, its double-tiered, white-columned piazza (echoed but not repeated by the half-circle porch on the west end of the house) all express an ideal of openness and hospitality. The curvature of the lunette on the third story, of the roundels on either side of the front steps, and of the side porch are small but important elements in this impression of grace.

The Manigault mansion is neither a Single House nor a Double House but a made-to-order design that deliberately departs from these two standard Charleston patterns. Rather than filling up a narrow city lot and having a garden and piazza hidden from public view, this house has plenty of room around it. It is less obsessed with privacy than the typical town house. As grand country houses tend to do, it wants to sweep the passerby inside. In a sense this is a country house that has moved to town but sits far to the north of Broad Street, Charleston's own Mason-Dixon line. The unique qualities of 350 Meeting Street derive from the mind of its architect, Gabriel Manigault, who built the house for his brother Joseph by 1806. Taking the house as a testimonial to the character of the builders, it would be fair to assume that they were openhanded men who held no grudges and were true to the sentiment on their family crest.

Gabriel Manigault was one of the first American architects, as distinct from the

The twin chimneys, double verandas, and bowed porch on the side of the house suggest a luxurious interior and add to the overall impression of balance and grace. Designed about 1803 by Gabriel Manigault, the house is Adamesque in style and may reflect French as well as English influences.

master-carpenters of the eighteenth century. His training, however, was in the law rather than in anything resembling engineering or design. He was an amateur as Thomas Jefferson was—in the grand, forgotten sense of that word. Architecture was one of several subjects that cultivated minds naturally turned to in these times. Gabriel Manigault learned his craft, just as Jefferson did, by reading the architectural handbooks of the day and by analyzing well-designed buildings. He designed not only this town house but another one (no longer standing) for himself, and two of the most beautiful of Charleston's surviving Federal-period buildings are attributed to him as well, the South Carolina Society Hall and what is now city hall, both of which are still in use.

When a visiting Irish artist, Walter Robertson, painted this miniature of him in 1794, Gabriel Manigault, age thirty-six, was a prominent planter and legislator.

In about 1803, when Gabriel designed this house for his brother, both were at the heart of power and influence in Charleston, rich planters and the scions of a notable Charleston family. Among their relations and in-laws were Middletons, Draytons, Izards, and Heywards, who by the late eighteenth century had become some of Charleston's most powerful families. Gabriel had greeted the American Revolution with no particular enthusiasm and spent most of the war years in England, reading law at Lincoln's Inn. But at home Joseph had gone to the front lines at the age of fifteen, accompanied by his grandfather, to defend Charleston against the British. Gabriel and Joseph both sat in the South Carolina convention that ratified the Constitution in 1788, and Gabriel served several terms in the state legislature. The brothers had inherited large holdings of land and slaves. Both had married well—Gabriel to an Izard and Joseph to Maria Middleton and then, after her early death, to Charlotte Drayton.

The interior of the mansion where Joseph and Charlotte lived is spacious and filled with light, the Southern home of one's daydreams. The wide stair hall, divided by a sweeping arch, is formed by a rectangle and semicircle. It is a very grand space;

The columns of the bowed porch make a frame for the circular gatehouse with its classical portico and pediment—a design borrowed from the small, round Roman temples so appealing to eighteenth-century taste. Artfully planned, seemingly artless vistas such as this were a feature of baroque architecture.

yet when all the doors are open, it has the charm of an old-fashioned breezeway. Beyond the arch the stairs turn majestically upward, seemingly unsupported by anything but the banister. Built in the same style as the staircase in the Nathaniel Russell house (Chapter Three), this one is solider and less precarious. The first landing is roomy, and light pours through the Palladian window there.

On the ground floor, to the left of the front entrance, are the library and what may have been a music room, and to the right a stately dining room, one end of which curves outward. Upstairs are a ballroom or drawing room of royal dimensions, a card room, and a bedroom with a luxurious adjunct that most Charleston town houses lacked—a separate dressing room. (On the third floor were other bedrooms, perhaps for the children and their nurses.)

The all-night drinking bout, actually conducted behind locked doors to block escape, was a custom much favored by Colonial gentlemen. At this party in 1760, Peter Manigault (father of Gabriel and Joseph) was the host.

The style of the decoration is Adamesque, that is, an American version of late-eighteenth-century English classicism. It is ornate but in the clean and controlled English manner; it embodies the intricacies and curves of late Greek and Roman interior design that so caught the imagination of the Scottish architect and decorator Robert Adam. He translated them for his lordly patrons in England; in this house his work is filtered through the sensibilities of a Charleston architect. Thus the house is not only American but English and Roman.

The Manigault family, one of the great clans of South Carolina, had been French, as their name reveals, part of the first wave of French settlers who came to South Carolina in the late seventeenth century. They were Huguenots, as French

Opposite: The elliptical wall of the dining room echoes and balances the bowed porch on the opposite side of the house. The woodwork and the curving cornices with their plaster urns and swags, characteristic of the Adamesque style, make the room exuberant and light. The three-part dining table is a Charleston piece of the early nineteenth century; the silver epergne at its center is by Paul Storr, a leading English silversmith.

Overleaf: One of the sideboards displays a fine set of early-nineteenth-century silver. The coffee urn at center was made by Boyce, a New York firm. The portrait, by an unknown artist, is of a Philadelphia lady.

Protestants were called, and they came not primarily for land and profits but out of religious motives or at least out of the desire to survive. In Catholic France the Protestants had faced annihilation. In 1598 Henry IV, who had converted to Catholicism in order to become king, had signed an edict of toleration in favor of the Protestants, the Edict of Nantes. But Henry's grandson Louis XIV reverted to orthodoxy and in 1685 canceled the edict. The Huguenots fled to Holland and England, and hundreds eventually crossed the Atlantic and settled in Charleston, which offered religious freedom. Among the émigrés was a young woman named Judith Giton, who reached the New World in 1685. The voyage took many months, and, because pestilence broke out on shipboard, Judith's aged mother died en route. Disembarking in Charleston, Judith had been obliged to work eight months to earn the twenty-four crowns she still owed for her passage. Then she married a fellow refugee, a weaver by trade, and after his death wed another of her compatriots, Pierre Manigault, the father of the dynasty.

The ivory button in the newel post of the main staircase may be a memento of brotherly love, placed there by Joseph and Gabriel Manigault as a sign of their cooperation. Or it may be a "mortgage button," symbolizing that the mansion was debt free.

Following this second marriage Judith Giton wrote a remarkable letter home to France—a letter emblematic of the lives of women in Colonial America, as well as a reminder of just how the first American fortunes were built. Judith recounted that even after her indenture was over, she had had many troubles to face. Her brother who had accompanied her to America had died of a fever, "not being fitted to the harsh work to which we were exposed. We have seen ourselves since our departure

Opposite: The glass-and-metal lighting fixture (a detail from the central hall) hangs from the ceiling above the stairwell. Of the same period as the house, it is probably French or Venetian.

Overleaf: The central hall and stairs combine rectangular and semicircular spaces for an Adamesque masterpiece. Beyond the archway the stairs rise in an easy curve, with the first landing meant to provide a vista of the house. In back of the stairs, to accommodate guests dismounting from carriages, is a double-doored second entrance. To the left stands a breakfront bookcase desk made in Salem, Massachusetts for the Manigault family.

from France, in every sort of affliction; sickness, pestilence, famine, poverty, very hard work. I was in this country a full six months, without tasting bread, and whilst I worked the ground, like a slave...." But now, she reported, God had had mercy on her, and her lot was happier. The starving times, she hoped, were ended.

As Pierre Manigault's wife, Judith took in boarders and cooked for them; Pierre operated a distillery and made whiskey barrels. Their joint efforts in the food-and-drink business laid the economic foundations for the mansion on Meeting Street, though neither of them could have imagined any such thing. Judith died in 1711 when her son Gabriel was only seven. This same Gabriel—the grandfather of the architect Gabriel and of Joseph—became a merchant and prospered. But his bent was philanthropy, and he gave a great deal of his money away in such causes as establishing a library for Charleston and educating the children of the poor. During the Revolutionary War he lent the state of South Carolina $220,000. And it was he who, at age seventy-five, volunteered for active duty with his grandson Joseph.

The family fortunes, in the next generation, passed into rice plantations, slaves, and real estate. When Joseph Manigault settled down to raise his family in his splendid new mansion on Meeting Street, he was truly an aristocrat and a gentleman—the more so, perhaps, because his great-grandparents had lived so plainly. The family had had no time to grow bored with gentlemanly occupations. Dreading the fevers of the rice country, Joseph visited his plantations as seldom as possible. He and Charlotte Manigault spent their days happily in their spacious home, watching over their ten children. Gabriel, meanwhile, had sold off his Charleston possessions and moved to Philadelphia. He and Joseph kept up with each other by mail. "Dear Brother," wrote Joseph in January 1806, "... I do not know any place where there are worse fires kept, than in Charleston. We have had a few days of remarkably cold weather, which, I take for granted, began first with you; the water has been several days frozen in a bason [sic] in a little North-West dressing-room, which I have appropriated to myself." (As in other Southern homes, people were amply prepared for hot summers but not for freezing winters.)

Joseph died in 1843, having outlived Gabriel by some years. He bequeathed his worldly goods to his widow, including the mansion, which she sold. It went through many hands, finally becoming a multifamily dwelling with many more than ten children under its roof. During World War II the government leased it as a U.S.O., and the house that had once no doubt dispensed Madeira and cakes offered coffee and doughnuts to soldiers. The Charleston Museum owns the Manigault house now

MANIGAULT HOUSE

The bedroom, which is plainer than the public rooms, is furnished with a typical Charleston bed, with rice sheaves carved on its posts. Instead of rope the mattress is held in place by slats, an innovation of Charleston cabinetmakers. For summer comfort the headboard is removeable. The mahogany-and-satinwood desk on the right is a Charleston-made piece of the period.

and has carefully restored it to its present state.

Judith and Pierre Manigault of course had no idea that their courage and hard labor would have such results as they had: that their son would grow up to be a philanthropist and patriot, or that one of their great-grandsons would rise to be a famous architect. But like Judith the whole family seems to have been writers and keepers of records. One of Gabriel's daughters kept a diary, and imagine what Great-Great-Grandmother Judith might have thought of this account of a day in the life of Miss Manigault, circa 1814: "After breakfast I translate French into English... I then walk up and down the music room while I read... I play the harp for another half hour." After listening to her mother read the Bible, the young lady was then free to do as she pleased, perhaps to play the piano for a while, or nap, or beautify herself for dinner. She ended this particular diary entry with the thought that her happiness was too great to last.

In 1831, many years after his father's death, Gabriel's son Charles Manigault, a world traveler, had this fashionable portrait made of himself, his wife, and their two small sons.

As she wrote these words, she was scarcely a century removed from the great-great-grandparents who had worked hard to have enough to eat. In such details, from the very hands of the people who experienced them, and in houses such as the one on Meeting Street, lies the history of not only one Charleston family but of the United States. Not all immigrants' hopes found such abundant fulfillment, but Manigault House, and the pioneer woman's letter, are ready evidence that some succeeded magnificently.

Opposite: One of the largest and most gracious in the city, the drawing room fills the western end of the house and opens onto both piazzas, allowing guests to move around freely and the summer breezes to fill the room. The south wall, where the gilt, Adam-style looking glass hangs, is exactly like the north.

Overleaf: The French console in gilded wood and the rococo side chairs (Italian-made in the Louis XV style) are handsome reminders of the French origins of the Manigault family. The silk draperies pool on the floor (or puddle or wallow, according to one usage or another)—a sign of lavishness and wealth.

OBJECTS OF GRACE

Charleston silver is rare, for on at least two occasions—after the British occupation of 1780–1782 and again during the Civil War—much of it was carried away and melted down. But prominent Charlestonians did acquire a great deal of silver plate: in the mid-eighteenth century it was not unusual for a wealthy family to own more than one thousand ounces. Silver provided both status and a convenient form of cash, since coins could be melted down and worked into a handsome piece that was useful and certainly more charming. Local smiths were eager to render such a service. John Ewan, one of the most prolific, advertised silver items "made to order, with neatness and dispatch." Like most of his fellow craftsmen, he was extraordinarily dexterous, fashioning pieces ranging from thimbles to imposing tableware such as the sugar bowl opposite.

The rich also turned to sources outside Charleston, especially London and established centers in the North such as Philadelphia. Even local tableware copied English models, from the chaste rococo and neoclassical styles of the eighteenth century to the grand elaborate forms of the nineteenth that utilized a multitude of motifs and much cast ornament. As styles proliferated, so did the amount of plate in a household, prompted in part by the wide use of sideboards for displaying special pieces. Given their sheen and appealing shapes, the examples on these pages would have appeared unquestionably superb.

S-shaped handles offset the rather squat contours of this inverted pear-shaped sugar bowl made by John Ewan in the nineteenth century and now in the Charleston Museum. The details are exquisite: cast bands of thistles and of acanthus encircle the base and body, while a mushroom finial tops the double-domed lid.

This John Ewan pitcher, an example of late-Empire-style silver, bears a repoussé cartouche (enclosing the initials SLN) and a scrolled handle with an appliqué scallop at its base (in detail opposite).

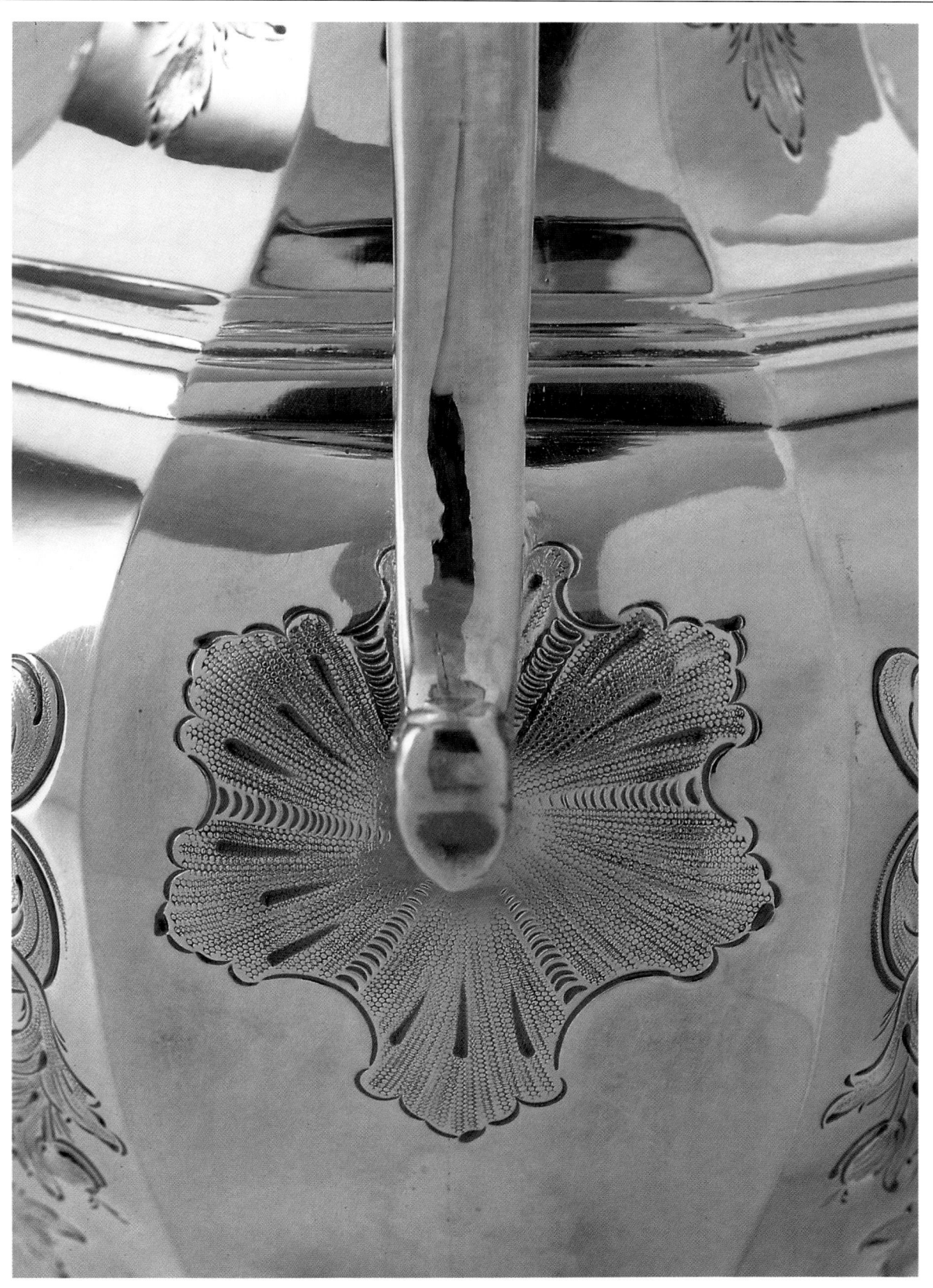

A Philadelphia firm of silversmiths, Bailey & Company, crafted this discreetly decorated six-piece tea and coffee service for Charles Alston, owner of the Edmondston-Alston house (Chapter Four), where these objects and the ones on pages 74–77 still reside. Each of the pieces here—a teapot and coffeepot, two pitchers, and covered and uncovered sugar bowls—bears the initials CA as well as the Alston crest.

A cruet stand in rococo form holds three silver casters (for salt, pepper, and mustard or catsup) and three silver-covered glass cruets (for oil, vinegar, and another condiment). Philadelphia silversmiths made the set for Charles Alston, whose family crest is engraved on the stand's cartouche, in detail opposite.

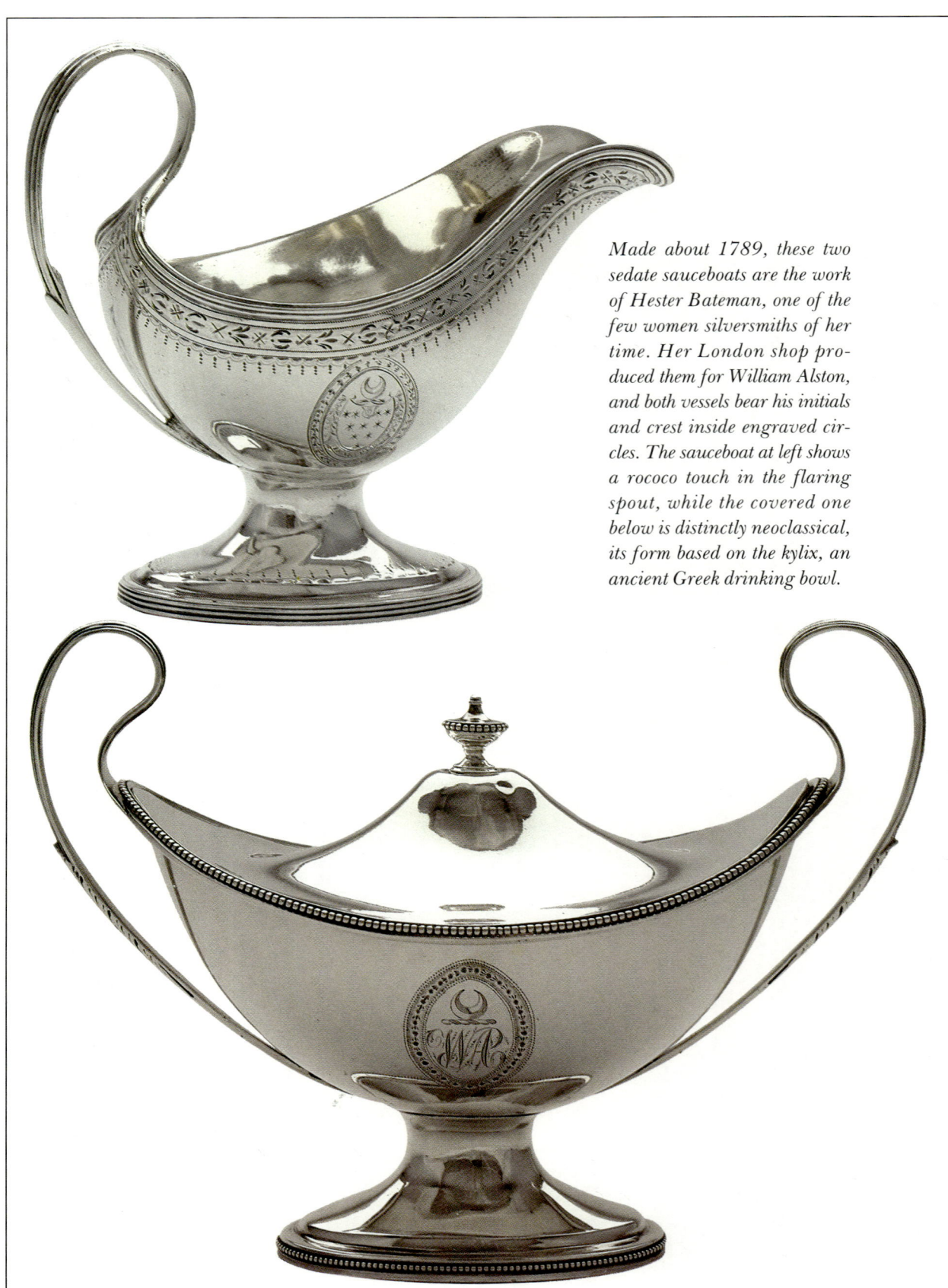

Made about 1789, these two sedate sauceboats are the work of Hester Bateman, one of the few women silversmiths of her time. Her London shop produced them for William Alston, and both vessels bear his initials and crest inside engraved circles. The sauceboat at left shows a rococo touch in the flaring spout, while the covered one below is distinctly neoclassical, its form based on the kylix, an ancient Greek drinking bowl.

This sumptuous epergne belonging to the Alston family was fashioned about 1818 by a London silversmith and served as the centerpiece for an ornately set dining table. The central bowl, resting on four fluted columns, might have held such delicacies as pickles, capers, or sweetmeats. Four smaller bowls—on graceful arms extending from beneath a pineapple finial—contained salt, pepper, dry mustard, and similar necessities.

A finely cast Grecian face peers out from a trail of vine leaves in this detail from the epergne on the previous page. These embellishments, like the massive form of the whole piece, were prominent features of Regency silver, the leading neoclassical style in England from 1790 to the 1840s.

One of the most lavish pieces of Southern silver is this wine wagon made about 1850 by Samuel Wilmot, who worked in the Charleston area and in Georgia. Used for serving wine, the wagon belonged to MEJ—the initials inside the cartouche—and displays outstanding castwork, particularly the wheel spokes and the two handles, one an elaborate scroll, the other a proud eagle.

3
NATHANIEL RUSSELL HOUSE
A NEST OF ROSES

The British peers who founded Charleston, or, more accurately, put up the capital to found it, intended to foster an aristocratic society, and Charleston has always endeavored to be one. Family names, in this place, are everything. But while the house of Nathaniel Russell is now a landmark, its builder was not an aristocrat in the Charleston sense. He came from Bristol, Rhode Island, and settled in Charleston in 1765, a bachelor of twenty-seven. His family at home was prominent in politics and the law, Russell himself a merchant. For all that pedigrees mattered in Charleston, society was still fluid, and money talked. A rich merchant, even a Yankee merchant, could rise quickly to the top. And if he had done nothing else, the handsome house that Russell built on Meeting Street in 1808 would have gained him absolution.

With understandable pride the first owner ordered his initials to be rendered in iron and set onto the balcony above the door.

The Russell house had no known professional architect and yet is an extraordinary building. A three-story brick dwelling with a fanlight above the broad front entrance and wrought-iron balconies outside the upper windows, the house is an odd one for Charleston. In a city of houses that typically sit side by side, this one withdraws upon its own large plot, within a copious garden. It is neither a Single House nor a Double House, and it has no piazza. Yet it resembles a Single House, being one room wide with a rectangular plan and, instead of a piazza, a four-sided bay on the south side. The front door opens into a large reception room,

A visitor to Nathaniel Russell House in its heyday described it as a "splendid mansion, surrounded by a wilderness of flowers, and bowers of myrtles"; it retains the same beguiling character now. The hexagonal wing, which creates the oval rooms of the house, juts into the garden on the left.

which Russell probably used for meeting business associates.

Through a pair of elaborate doors, the reception room opens into a stair hall, where the glory of this house is revealed, one of the loveliest pieces of woodwork in the city—a famous "flying" staircase. It curves upward to the top floor in a spiral that never touches the walls, and, like some delicate bridge suspended high above a gorge, it is a tour de force, meant to make the viewer gasp.

Nathaniel Russell was eighty when this miniature was painted in 1818, two years before his death. It now sits on the dressing table of the bedroom upstairs.

In the unusual floor plan of this house, each floor has three main rooms and each room its own shape: one of them square, one rectangular, and (within the four-sided bay), one oval. On the first floor the oval room is the library, and on the second floor a music room of considerable elegance. The rooms are an exceptional example of the Adamesque style. Robert Adam, the famous Scottish architect, took his inspiration from exuberant late Roman interiors, and here—in the carving of the woodwork, the classical motifs, the garlands, the pilasters that frame the windows and the mirrors in the music room—is an American version of the Adamesque style.

Not only in the decoration does the spirit of Robert Adam come into play, but also in the alternation of shapes and sizes of the rooms, the height of the windows, and the cascading stairway. All these elements, as well as the light that pours in the windows, give the house a sense of gaiety, a quality of surprise. Though elegant in every respect, it has nothing of Georgian solidity about it. Perhaps it is not Russell's preferences that are so strongly reflected here but those of his wife and daughters, for there is a strong sense of femininity about this house—in the grace of the stairway, in the lyrical frets and flourishes of the wood carving. On the first landing of the staircase today hangs the portrait of a Charleston lady in a lavish gown. She is

Opposite: On the first landing of the spectacular staircase hangs an oil done in 1786 by George Romney, the celebrated London portraitist. The lady is Mary Rutledge Smith. Though she did not live in this house, she was a prominent Charlestonian and a grande dame of the late Colonial period.

Overleaf: In this view from the third floor, the cantilevered staircase descends, without apparent support, in a series of graceful ellipses resembling the spiraling of a shell. The curves, the lightness, and the daring typify the Adamesque style, which manages to be dignified as well as flamboyant.

exactly the right spirit to preside over it.

Nathaniel Russell had come to Charleston to seek his fortune, and as a dealer in rice and indigo, cotton and rum, sugar, oil, and slaves, he had found it in abundance. As any intelligent merchant might, he went in for politics, too. He was obviously a deliberate man, who took his time when it came to important things. In 1788 when he decided to marry, he was only five months short of his fiftieth birthday, and the wife he chose—Sarah Hopton, a spinster of thirty-five—was the daughter of his business partner. Luckily for a couple so advanced in years, their progeny arrived without complications, Alicia the next year and Sarah in 1791. The family lived in comfortable circumstances on East Bay near the warehouses. As the years passed, Russell watched his assets accumulate and laid his plans to build a house that Charleston would notice. His daughters were approaching marriageable age and might as well marry old money and old names. A fine new house could hardly harm these prospects. Before 1808 construction at 51 Meeting Street was begun. Russell spent eighty thousand dollars on the house and its furnishings, an unimaginable sum for the times.

The Green Drawing Room on the second floor, an ample rectangular space that served as the formal parlor, is filled with sunlight. The woodwork, ornamented with neoclassical motifs, is original. The tea table is set with French china.

Surely there is something to the story that Russell built the staircase in the hope of seeing Alicia and Sarah descend it in their wedding dresses. His dreams, of course, tended to come true. In 1809, when the paint in the new mansion could scarcely have been dry, Alicia married Arthur Middleton of Bolton Plantation on the Stono River, who not only brought a great fortune to his bride but also one of the

---

Opposite: In this detail of the drawing room, an oil painting (perhaps part of Russell's collection) of cherubs by the seventeenth-century Italian Francesco Albani hangs above an Italian console.

Overleaf: Fine Charleston-made pieces furnish the dining room on the first floor. The Hepplewhite table is set with silver and with Chinese export porcelain. The oil painting above the massive sideboard is by an anonymous Dutch artist of the seventeenth century. Each floor of the house has a square, an oval, and a rectangular room; the dining room, now somewhat enlarged, was originally square.

most distinguished names in America. The Middletons had come from England to Barbados to Charleston in the seventeenth century: one of the family served as Colonial governor, and later Middletons became leaders of the American Revolution. Arthur Middleton's uncle had signed the Declaration of Independence. And in 1813 Sarah Russell married the Right Reverend Theodore Dehon, rector of St. Michael's Church, which stood only a few doors up Meeting Street. Like her father, the Reverend Theodore Dehon was a transplanted Rhode Islander, as well as rector of this powerful church and Episcopal bishop of South Carolina. Thus, beneath the roof of an extravagant new mansion, commerce joined hands with church and state. At the time his second daughter married, Russell was seventy-five, an age when other men were patting the curls of their great-grandchildren.

The Reverend Theodore Dehon unfortunately died only four years after he had married Sarah, and she returned to live with her parents, bringing her three children with her. An English traveler came to Charleston about this time and noted in his diary, "Called on the venerable Nathaniel Russell, Esq., residing in a splendid mansion, surrounded by a wilderness of flowers, and bowers of myrtles, oranges, and lemons, smothered with fruit and flowers." He spoke of visiting the Russells at home on another occasion, "living in a nest of roses." The women of the household were devoted gardeners, and the garden, according to the account of one Russell descendant, "occupied half a block and was filled with every imaginable plant and flower."

Nathaniel Russell died in 1820, almost eighty-two. "He was a native of New England, an honor to the land which gave him birth and a blessing to this city," his obituary ran. His widow and his widowed daughter continued to live in the house together, and from that time onward the house was chiefly the abode of women.

As her role evolved in the nineteenth century, the Charleston woman (except for the brief years when she was of marrying age) lived a sequestered and often lonely life. Colonial women and Revolutionary women had occasionally attained a kind of independence, but the definition of ladylike behavior narrowed in the nineteenth

Opposite: The mirrors in the music room (overleaf) are framed by horizontally fluted Corinthian pilasters, and the frieze above features gilded palmettes and flowers: Adamesque woodwork in the highest style.

Overleaf: The curving walls of the smaller second-floor drawing room, now fitted out as a music room, add to its festive air, as do the windowlike mirrors, designed to catch every flicker of candlelight or sunshine: a nineteenth-century method of making the most of light. The harp was made by Sébastien Erard in Paris in about 1803, the Récamier couch in New York at about the same time.

century. As one Charleston author described it, woman was "a being of sentiment and love, folding her affections around the other sex, animating his nature, and infusing into his heart the wholesome lessons of peace. Unlike the women of other times, who were masculine and sensual, she possesses the responsibilities of a moral agent...." She was a queen but only in the home, "wherein she shines most, and is everywhere else a stranger.... She cannot go into the world like the other sex."

Managing an establishment like Russell House must have been an exacting job; yet the servants did most everything. Married ladies were not expected to go out in public, and widows certainly not. Spinsters, too, were unwelcome in society, and pregnant women were not even allowed to sit in church. Goddesses of the hearth though they might have been, there must have been many a dreary afternoon when the ladies of Charleston had no diversion but embroidery or the tea table. The year after Nathaniel Russell died, the two Sarahs, mother and daughter, founded an organization called the Female Domestic Missionary Society. Its purpose was not to carry Christ to the heathen, as the title suggests, but to provide a place where the widowed, the pregnant, and women too poor to rent pews in the society churches might go to worship on Sundays.

Thomas Middleton, kinsman of the Arthur Middleton who married one of the Russell daughters, painted this group of gentlemen-musicians in Charleston about 1835–1840. Musicales such as this must have been common in this talented family.

In the late 1850s, after both Sarah Russells had died, their house was sold to the governor of South Carolina, Robert F. W. Allston, and next it went to a religious order, the Sisters of Charity of Our Lady of Mercy, who turned it into a convent school. Since in those times little girls were very well behaved, the sisters probably did not have to tell them to keep off the banister and not to clatter up and down the stairs. In 1908 the house passed once more into private hands and then in 1955

Opposite: The bed, New York made in the Sheraton style, is dressed out in white dimity and muslin for the summer months. The cradle is English and the rug Chinese. The Carolina summer called for seasonal changes in hangings and floor covering. To keep out mosquitoes, beds were draped in gauze.

Overleaf: The oval room on the first floor is the library now but was listed as a bedroom in 1857. It is dominated by two massive George I chairs that are among the finest English or Irish imports surviving in America. They belonged to the Colonial plantation house Drayton Hall, near Charleston.

became the property and headquarters of the Historic Charleston Foundation.

Nathaniel Russell built this house for his wife and daughters and no doubt would hardly mind that it seems more their monument than his. Every house in Charleston reflects the centuries that have passed over it, the people that have lived in it, and is marked perhaps by hurricane or earthquake or war. Since so many of the town houses mirror the ideals and aspirations of the gentleman, Russell House can very well stand as the homeplace of the Charleston lady, "a person...of sentiment, not of appetite...timid, confiding, submissive." If such a creature existed, this house would have made a decorative setting for her, as she poured tea, smiled at her children, and perhaps strummed a few ladylike measures on the harp.

With its chandeliers lighted and its door thrown open, Russell House looks almost as it might have on a summer evening in 1815. The front entrance has a floral fanlight. The ornamental double doors behind the reception room table conceal the stair hall and its famous staircase.

FURNITURE IN THE BEST MANNER

Charleston's stately town houses created such a great demand for furniture that the city became the preeminent furniture-making center of the South: nearly 250 cabinetmakers worked in Charleston between 1700 and 1825. Their first choice of material was mahogany, a wood easy to obtain from the West Indies. Using it in combination with local woods such as cypress, they sculpted furniture in "the best manner," as a 1734 advertisement promised. Among their creations are the pieces on the following pages, all of which are now in Heyward-Washington House (Chapter One) unless noted otherwise.

The insistence on excellence and productivity is manifested in the career of Thomas Elfe, the city's most famous cabinetmaker. In one eight-year period, from 1768 to 1775, Elfe's workshop turned out some 1,500 items, from double chests of drawers such as the one on page 112 to picture frames. Much of the furniture produced by Elfe and other Charlestonians follows English styles, notably Thomas Chippendale's and, after the Revolution, the neoclassical fashions of George Hepplewhite. To these the Charlestonians added their own flourishes, such as the carved fret on page 108. No Charleston "school" as such has emerged: these early craftsmen were quick to adopt new styles, and they did not identify their work. But what came from their hands was some of the finest furniture made in the South, or anywhere.

Made by an unknown Charleston cabinetmaker about 1770, this magnificent library bookcase is one of the great pieces of Colonial furniture. It measures nearly eleven feet high and more than eight feet wide, and the texture and matching of the mahogany in its five sections are superb, as are the inlay work, the veneering on the base, and the secondary woods (details pages 104–107). The bookcase may also have been used to display ceramics.

Adding to the charm of the bookcase on page 103 are the brass fittings and the drawer linings of cypress.

Deftly carved scrolls inlaid with satinwood and tipped with bellflowers flow across the bookcase's pediment.

An ivory bellflower from the veneered base has veins that were scratched in and darkened with lampblack.

The handsome mahogany table below, a drop-leaf breakfast table made about 1770 and now at Middleton Place north of Charleston, is attributed to Thomas Elfe. The basic design comes from Chippendale, but the masterfully pierced and carved fretwork on the skirt, in detail above, is Elfe's distinguishing mark.

Its top tilted up for storing against a wall, this round scallop-edged mahogany table in Russell House is a splendid example of a form of tea table popular with fashionable eighteenth-century Charlestonians.

These elegant chairs epitomize how Charleston cabinetmakers interpreted two famous English styles of seating. The mahogany side chair at left, made between 1760 and 1780 for a plantation house, is in the Rococo Chippendale manner: scrolls and leafage cover much of it, and it is supported in front by cabriole legs that end in paw-and-ball feet. The armchair opposite, crafted of mahogany, ash, and yellow pine in about 1790, has the shield-shaped back, tapered legs, and crisp lines typical of Hepplewhite-style furniture.

More than six feet tall, the double chest of drawers at left, attributed to Thomas Elfe, is admirably proportioned and glows with fine details. The pattern and color of the brasses complement the plain mahogany drawer fronts, while a carved frieze around the top section and fluted columns along the lower sides form a precise frame. The unit was made in the early 1770s.

The mahogany clothespress opposite is a late-eighteenth-century piece made in Charleston and now in Middleton Place. Beneath an imposing pediment, doors open to disclose five movable trays for laying away folded clothing—here, period garments made in London for members of the Middleton family.

Dark-grained mahogany contrasts with lighter satinwood inlays in this detail from a Charleston bookcase.

An interlaced diamond and figure eight form the center of this splat on a chair attributed to Thomas Elfe.

4
EDMONDSTON-ALSTON HOUSE
OLD TIMES AND OKRA SOUP

The house at 21 East Battery is by no means the oldest or the most lavish dwelling south of Broad Street. But its shady, triple-storied piazza, supported by rows of classical columns, and its situation right on the harbor give it the air of the quintessential Charleston house. Its interiors, at the same time, have a homey and intimate quality that visitors sense and like. One could move into this house, be comfortable in it, savor the quiet pleasures of a summer afternoon on the breeze-swept piazza. There are small secrets everywhere, if the visitor knows where to look for them. This building bears the history not only of its inhabitants but of Charleston itself.

The Edmondston-Alston house is named for the man who built it and the family who lived in it the longest. In 1799 a young Scotsman, Charles Edmondston, came to Charleston to start a business, one of many enterprising immigrants eager to find a place among the older Carolina aristocrats. Edmondston traded his way to wealth in

This East Battery home was originally much plainer. In 1838 Charles Alston remodeled it in the Greek Revival style and also installed gas lighting. The cast-iron balcony was added after an older one was shaken down in the earthquake of 1886.

As part of his remodeling plan in 1838, Charles Alston added a third story to the existing piazza, embellishing the new tier with a row of Corinthian columns that contrast with the Doric ones below. The Corinthian order pleasantly echoes the shape of the palmettos and palms below.

cotton, a relatively new commodity in Charleston in the nineteenth century. He acquired sailing ships of his own, and a wharf, and a family. In 1828 he built a fine waterfront home for himself and his wife on this East Battery site, which had hitherto been Cooper River marshland. Now, thanks to a recently constructed seawall, it had become solid ground for a house.

The plan he chose was an eccentric one, neither a Single House nor a Double, but something wide and airy, with a front door that opened into a wide hall, which led into yet another hall at right angles, which in turn gave access to the staircase on the north wall and to the piazza on the south. Downstairs were two important rooms—the reception room and the dining room. On the second floor, as befitted a man of his station, he put double drawing rooms of noble proportions, which were separated by an oval hall, and a library, and on the third floor the bedrooms.

The window's shutters at the first landing are open here, but Charleston custom dictated that north-side windows should stay shuttered, since they often looked into the south-side piazza of the house next door.

But cotton proved a treacherous source of riches, and the boom of the late 1820s turned sour in the next decade. In 1838, finding himself bankrupt with $125,000 worth of unpayable debts, Edmondston had to sell his house and most of its contents. And as though the older aristocracy of Charleston wished to reassert its primacy over the self-made and the nouveau riche, the Edmondston house passed to the possession of William Alston, one of the lordliest of all Carolina planters. Already the owner of the Miles Brewton house on King Street, William Alston bought the house on East Battery for his son Charles.

The mythology of the Southern gentleman—presumably blue blooded, rich, civilized, and wise—has taken a beating in recent times. But "King Billy" Alston, as his admirers called him, was the genuine article. His possessions were awe inspiring:

The two entrance hallways of the house converge at the staircase, here in detail, which leads upward to the library and the drawing room. The nicely turned posts and the carefully carved scrolls of the risers are the kind of painstaking detail that characterizes this house. The statuette is on the first landing.

more than 700 slaves, as well as real estate, bank stocks, racing stables, and a library of 250 books. One of his in-laws observed of him that he could always be found "in the neighborhood of Race-horses and Democrats, two species of animals, you know, he is fond of." He was also fond of his numerous progeny, by two successive wives. Charles, for whom he bought the house, was one of six children by the second wife. Alston saw to it that his sons by his first wife went to Princeton, and the second batch to Yale.

In spite of having hired an expensive tutor, Charles failed to graduate from Yale, returning happily to South Carolina to become a planter like his father. By 1838 he had reached the age of forty-two and acquired a wife (Emma Pringle, of another distinguished family) and four children, ranging in age from two to ten. Charles Alston was undoubtedly pleased with his father's purchase, which he proceeded to remodel in the latest style, adding a third story to the piazza, as well as Corinthian columns and a significant amount of interior woodwork. Like William Roper, whose house was only a few doors away (Chapter Five), Charles Alston was enamored of the Greek Revival style and wanted his home to reflect the prevailing decorative trend.

Perhaps because so many of the furnishings in the house at present actually belonged to the Alston family, they convey a vivid sense of homelife, even an aura of what must have been supremely happy years in the 1840s and 1850s. The Alston children were Joseph (the eldest), Charles, Susan, and John Julius. For the two youngest the lovely new house on the harbor would have formed their earliest childhood memories. By 1850 the two older boys were grown, but Susan was only eighteen and John Julius fourteen. Their parents were at the very heart of society, with connections of lineage and friendship to whole regiments of Manigaults, Middletons, Pringles, Haynes, Pinckneys, Brewtons, and Mottes.

A wonderfully revealing document in Emma Alston's own hand has survived these years: her cookbook, now preserved at the South Carolina Historical Society.

Opposite: The massive table in the dining room has fourteen legs and can be opened to accommodate additional leaves. It is set with family silver and Chinese export porcelain, which in the early nineteenth century usually arrived in Charleston as ballast in the holds of ships, packed under more valuable cargo.

Overleaf: The second-floor drawing room, with its view of the harbor, its windows framed in deeply cut pilasters, and its cast-iron balcony, is furnished today as a music room, which was always one of its uses. Except for the mantelpiece all the woodwork is original to the house, as are most of the furnishings.

It is a slim, homemade volume, its pages neatly stitched together, with "receipts" for cakes copied out on the same pages with directions for making horrendous amounts of lye soap. Mrs. Alston's script is decided and unwavering. She made no blot or error from beginning to end. And on the final page she lists, with evident pride, her menu for the Race Week ball in 1851. (Race Week was the social and emotional high point of the year.) She notes that she required six dozen wine glasses and "as many tumblers and champagne glasses as could be collected" and eighteen dozen plates. Her buffet was a feat of Carolina gastronomy consisting, in part, of four turkeys and four hams, sixty partridges, several braces of pheasants and ducks, and ten quarts of oysters.

On the usual weekdays Mrs. Alston set a splendid table also. One of her husband's nephews, writing his memoirs years later, recalled the joy of arriving at "Uncle Charles Alston's house on the Battery," where he could have a luxurious bath and then sit down to a "home dinner of okra soup first and a bottle of old Madeira last."

The house is full of other evidence of the tastes and habits of the Alston family. The library, with its fireplace and ingenious fire screen, which allowed the bookworm to toast his toes and at the same time protect his face from the heat, is one of the pleasantest rooms in Charleston. Racing calendars and studbooks sit beside the plays of Beaumont and Fletcher. Charles Alston collected art as well as books. *Quadrupeds*, the set of prints by John J. Audubon he purchased, are still in his drawing room. He owned a telescope for home use and was a traveler, too. In 1859 Susan and his eldest son accompanied him to Europe, where he had his daughter's portrait done in pastels. It hangs now in the dining room, but there is another, better picture of her, a daguerreotype (now kept in a drawer at the house) made about the time she came back from the Grand Tour. She is beautifully gowned and wears a chic Paris hat. She is the very image of the Charleston belle, well mannered and observant of every propriety. The portrait is haunting because it caught Susan Alston at the very moment of perfection—young, intelligent, with all the privileges and possessions that wealth and a pedigree conferred.

Only a few years hence, the family telescope would be put to an ominous use: through it General P.G.T. Beauregard watched the bombardment of Fort Sumter.

French doors open onto the second floor of the piazza, making an ideal vantage point for a tea table, which every drawing room had, along with an elaborate tea service. Visitors to Charleston described tea time as the most pleasant of the day. Music and conversation abounded, along with tea and sweets.

Though neither the general nor Charles Alston would have believed it, this dubious triumph was of course the first step toward disaster. Southern patriots that they were, the Alstons spent the war years on their plantation, growing rice to feed the Confederate Army. John Julius, the baby of the family, was twenty-four when the war began. He raised a company for Confederate service at his own expense and was commissioned a first lieutenant in the South Carolina Artillery.

Though some other houses on East Battery were reduced to desolate ruins in the final explosions that ended the war, the Alston house suffered fairly minor damage. Yet the war robbed the family of its drive. Susan Alston was well into her thirties when the war ended. She never married—indeed a generation of marriageable men was dead or maimed; widows and spinsters were everywhere. The surviving Alston brothers did not found families either. Susan inherited the town house and lived there with her servants, Julia (the cook) and John (the butler). After the manner of Southern gentlewomen, she always carried a little basket with her keys and some coins, and she always wore a lace cap. She never modernized: Julia and John cooked in the old kitchen out back on an open hearth. According to the recollection of a visitor, Susan always ate her dinner at three P.M., and it always began with okra soup. Tiny, shy, and reserved, Miss Susan Alston died in 1921 at the the age of eighty-nine. The house passed into a cousin's hands and today, carefully restored, is open to the public, who can imagine reading by the library fire or dancing reels in the drawing room; they may even (if they sniff the air) catch the aroma of okra soup.

In this daguerreotype Susan Alston, the last of her name to live here, wears a Paris hat and gown, probably acquired on her recent trip abroad with her father.

The library furnishings include a slant-top desk and an Empire-style settee, but its glory is the collection of a thousand-odd volumes reflecting the intellectual interests of the family. They studied Latin and Greek; read fiction, history, and poetry; and valued the modern along with the ancient.

AUDUBON IN CHARLESTON

Few renderings of natural wonders have been as acclaimed as the bird studies of John James Audubon. His monumental work, *The Birds of America,* contains 435 life-size engravings that still astonish artists and naturalists alike for their amazing faithfulness to living birds. Equally brilliant, but less well known, are the paintings from which the engravers worked. Audubon composed these, largely in watercolor, during some eighteen years of roaming the eastern United States, and one of his favorite sites was Charleston.

When he first arrived in 1831, he immediately met the Reverend John Bachman, a Lutheran minister who shared Audubon's love of birds and introduced him to other ardent naturalists among the Charleston gentry. "It is impossible to do justice to their extreme kindness toward me," reported the artist. The Charlestonians supplied him with specimens and joined him on hunts. Some of the paintings here are of birds he encountered around Charleston; others, showing Western birds, are paintings he completed in Charleston on several visits. Audubon seldom stayed in one place very long. But he and Bachman remained close friends for life, and it was to Bachman he once wrote, with a combination of vanity and prescience: "Assist me all you can.... My work will be studied for years to come."

LONG-BILLED CURLEW

A sea marsh off of Charleston is the setting for a pair of long-billed curlews, prairie birds that in Audubon's day migrated to the Carolina shores but are now rarely seen in the East. Audubon painted them in the fall of 1831, shortly after arriving in Charleston. An assistant, George Lehman, executed the background view of Charleston Harbor. The prominent round structure at left is Castle Pinckney, one of three island forts that guarded the harbor.

Audubon painted this snowy egret in the spring of 1832, during a stay at John Bachman's home. By late March, wrote Audubon, thousands of the birds had arrived in Charleston and "were seen in the marshes and rice fields, all in full plumage." For the background George Lehman added a plantation in the Carolina Low Country.

An adult male little blue heron shows off his spring plumage in a countryside habitat near Charleston. Audubon found this species especially lovely: "You may see the graceful heron, quietly and in silence walking along the margins of the water, with an elegance and grace which can never fail to please you." The partial inscription at upper right is evidently an instruction to Havell, a London engraver, for adding a second bird, which exists in pale outline just above the painted bird's back. In the engraving Havell did include a young heron in white plumage and also subtly altered the landscape.

BLACK-CROWNED NIGHT HERON

At dusk on a marsh, a black-crowned night heron darts at a frog near the claw of a smaller heron resting on one leg. Audubon composed this work at Charleston in June of 1832, using pencil and pastel as well as watercolor.

Five pairs of different species of woodpecker chatter and feed while clinging to tree limbs. Audubon drew the four birds at top about 1822; he finished the work in Charleston during the winter of 1836–1837.

Six types of warblers and bluebirds perch on a strawberry shrub in a work Audubon painted in Charleston. Assisted by his son John, he painted these predominently Western birds from an ornithologist's specimens.

SAGE GROUSE

In a painting completed in Charleston, a male sage grouse, on the right, courts a female by spreading his tail feathers and inflating his yellow esophagus. Audubon obtained specimens of these birds, whose home is the American Northwest, from members of the famous Lewis and Clark expedition.

SWAINSON'S HAWK

A swainson's hawk swoops down upon a marsh hare in a painting Audubon depicted from a specimen retrieved in the Northwest. The horned lizard on the left was removed for the engraving and a background put in.

5
ROPER HOUSE

A VIEW TO THE CANARIES

Roper House, built in 1838 by a wealthy planter, is one of the most flamboyant houses in Charleston, on one of the prime sites. In choosing the design for his handsome new dwelling, Robert William Roper did not record his purposes—or, if he did, the record has been lost. But if his house speaks accurately of him, he was a man to whom fashion mattered, a man who cared for appearances, for he chose to build not only a grand house but a notably modern one for its day, a lovely if eccentric work of Greek Revival architecture. Whatever Roper may have thought of the glory that was Greece, surely he was pleased to commission one of the first up-to-date houses in Charleston, to be among those who finally broke away from the Georgian-Adamesque styles of the past and took the long-overdue step out of the eighteenth century into the nineteenth.

Greek Revival was, of course, the favored building style of the young American republic, though in fact it was more a Roman revival than a Greek one. Architects in Boston, Philadelphia, and Washington eagerly borrowed the ground plan, the rows of columns, and the proportions of classical temples for the public buildings and the stately homes of the new nation. Their line of reasoning was that since the shining political ideals of Athens and of the Roman republic had been reincarnated here, America must have the architecture to match them. And so the colonnades arose in cities and in villages, and on the front porches of country manors.

Colonial architecture had also thrived on Greco-Roman allusions and decorations. But while the pediments and capitals and flutes and friezes of eighteenth-

The three-story brick facade and quiet front entrance might belong to a town house anywhere, but the white piazza with its tall columns above an arcade turns Roper House into a distinctly Charlestonian mansion and an elegant example of controlled but opulent architectural display.

century English architecture came from antiquity (as interpreted by the Italian Renaissance architects), they were very much the expression of English (or American) rationality. Classical flourishes were a shorthand denoting right-mindedness. No one quite connected classicism with radical politics. The Englishman loved Athenians because they were noble, not because they invented democracy. However, Thomas Jefferson, the genius of the new age of American architecture and a great promoter of the classical revival style, looked to the Romans because they had been republicans. But the truly satisfying part about the Greek Revival style was that, like other presumably sober republican fashions of the time, it easily succumbed to the uses of grandeur. Corinthian columns on the front of a house not only proclaimed that the occupant was the spiritual heir of Pericles and Cicero but announced in the same breath that he had plenty of money, too.

The dining room, of presidential dimensions, is furnished with American Empire antiques, including a table and chairs made in Boston about 1820. Behind the chandelier gleams a gilt-framed convex mirror, emblematic of the taste of the time.

By the late 1830s, when Charleston took up the trend, the Greek Revival style was no longer in the avant-garde. Charleston had been slow to change, probably because of the faltering Charleston economy. France and England had until 1814 been involved in a bitter war in both hemispheres, and the United States had been at war with England. Shipping had suffered, and there was no base for Charleston to fall back on. The old rice-and-indigo boom times had been dead for more than half a century, were as remote a memory as speakeasies are to us. While the North had industrial resources, the South had only cotton to export. And the more cotton they produced, the lower the price of it.

Thus, as the rest of America bloomed and expanded, Charleston began to struggle for its life. As an index to economic growth, in the years between 1800 and

In another view of the Roper house dining room, the table is set with English silver and china. Above the black marble mantelpiece hangs a portrait of Henry Clay, the famous Kentucky statesman and mediator. The doorway opens into the entrance hall to reveal Roper House's spiral staircase.

1860, the population of the United States increased sevenfold, from just over five million to thirty-five million—an astounding upsurge hardly matched on the face of the earth before or since. In those same decades the growth rate of Charleston was declining, and money was scarce. Nevertheless, this great port was far from being defunct. A man could still make his fortune in this harbor and on its docks. Roper House, along with a few other buildings of this epoch, stands as a symbol not only of its owner's social aspirations but of the vitality Charleston still possessed in the years before the Civil War.

The heavy table with lion-paw feet in the downstairs reception room is attributed to Joseph Meeks & Sons, nineteenth-century furniture makers. The French Empire chair with tapestry back and seat has the same solid, low-slung look as the table.

The portico of Roper House, a three-tiered mansion of brick, has that same beguiling twist of the older piazzas of Charleston: the soaring white columns and the porch they create are on the south side of the house, not across the front door where one would expect them to be in a house anywhere else. The relatively modest, mahogany, double front doors, framed with a rope-shaped molding that may recall the name of the owner, open quietly onto the street. The portico is the most eye-catching feature of the house; it is an odd piece of work. The volutes at the column capitals are carved in pure Ionic style, but the columns themselves are simple, uncarved cylinders, instead of being fluted all around. And there is either one column too many or one too few, for the number of columns in a portico should be even, dividing equally on either side of a doorway. But this, of course, is a piazza,

Opposite: With its neoclassical curves and claw feet, the Récamier couch in the downstairs reception room exemplifies the English Regency style of the early nineteenth century. The marble bust of the marquis de Lafayette is a copy of an original by the French sculptor Jean Antoine Houdon.

Overleaf: In this detail of the reception room, the curve of the Récamier couch with its lion-head ornament echoes the Grecian lyre that is on the chair back. The piece in the background, also in detail, is a tall secretary with fine brass fittings, probably the work of the New York firm of Joseph Meeks.

not a portico. Although the architect—and surely he was such, rather than a mere carpenter—was copying from a definite Greek model, he copied selectively.

Robert William Roper left no scrap of autobiography behind, but he had a reputation among his peers as a careful man with a dollar. "He was certainly fond of petty savings, which gave him the appearance of parsimoniousness," one of Roper's friends wrote of him, offering no explanation why this prudent temperament should have settled in an opulent, ostentatious house that stood, moreover, upon a piece of high-risk real estate. The Battery, as the easternmost rim of the Charleston peninsula is called, had been historically vulnerable to marauders of every description: from Spaniards in Colonial times plying northward from the Caribbean and Florida, usually looking for trouble, to the pirates and privateers that sailed the Bermuda triangle. The British eventually turned into Charleston's main threat. During the Revolutionary War the redcoats came both by land and by sea. In 1779 the British beat their way through the swamps and came in the back door, with a navy attacking the harbor as well. During the War of 1812—as Roper could no doubt recall—the Battery cannons had stood ready to fend off British warships.

In this view of the Battery in the late 1850s, Roper House is the four-columned structure at far right, the second house above the corner where East and South Battery meet. In those days, as now, the skyline was dominated by church steeples.

And besides marauders and belligerents, this point of land was at the mercy of high tides and hurricanes. But after 1814 the British were gone for good, and in the 1830s, after several attempts, the city at last constructed a permanent seawall. When the seawall was finished, the Battery quickly became the most desirable property in the city. The sea breeze was clean and strong, the views incomparable.

As Roper began to build his house at #9, he could look south all the way to the Ashley River, and across the Atlantic all the way to the Canary Islands (as a famous boast of the day had it), with nothing to mar the view except the small, malignant lump called Fort Sumter. It had sat on the Charleston seascape since only 1829, part of a chain of American coastal defenses. When the foundations of Roper House were laid, Martin Van Buren was president, and John C. Calhoun, formerly vice president and now senator from South Carolina, had repeatedly threatened secession over the tariff issue. Slavery was an even more agonizing issue between North and South. If Roper paid attention to politics, and as a responsible and wealthy South Carolinian he certainly did, he may well have reflected that Sumter's guns might fire one day. And although the new seawall provided some sense of security to the owners of seafront property, hurricanes still could and did rip off shutters, smash windows, and turn splendid new drawing rooms into mud seas and handsome staircases into sluiceways. But to Robert William Roper the hazards must have seemed worth braving, a fair wager against the chance to live in style at the correct address.

All that is known of him comes from the casual recollections of two of his acquaintances. Roper must have been very much a man of his time and place—a planter, a citizen, a gentleman. As a rice planter he was a part-time Charlestonian. He married a lady of excellent family connections, Martha Rutledge Laurens, whom he called Patsy. They loved each other tenderly, it was said, and unfortunately had no children. He undoubtedly held a sizable number of slaves, who worked his plantation and made his town house habitable. As is the habit of the Tidewater aristocracy, Roper traced his paternal lineage all the way back to William the Conqueror, in his case to a Norman invader named "de Ropere," and on the maternal side to Sir Thomas More.

According to one of Roper's friends, he was an intelligent man, given to self-improvement. But, contrary to all Southern notions of proper manners, he loved to show off what he knew and could never bring himself to quit. One day, as a distinguished citizen and member of the South Carolina state legislature, he delivered a patriotic oration on Sullivans Island. Such speeches, in the nineteenth century, tended to go on for at least two hours. The next afternoon friends of Mrs. Roper came to call at 9 East Battery, and Roper repeated the whole performance for them. On top of that Roper could not shake his reputation for tightfistedness. Yet he was laboring under a handicap, for he had no money he could call his own, his father having strictly entailed the Roper estate.

On April 12, 1861, all Charleston gathered on the rooftops to watch Confederate artillery drive the U.S. garrison from Fort Sumter. In 1865 Roper House was damaged by cannon fire.

Entailment, according to the English-derived inheritance laws of the time, enabled a man to keep control of his estate even after he was long dead. In *Pride and*

Prejudice what makes the plot go round is that Mr. Bennet's estate is entailed; that is, it cannot be inherited by any of his five daughters but only by his nonexistent sons. Robert Roper's father had put similar strictures on the family fortune. In the case that Robert produced no heirs, all the money had to go to the founding of a hospital. Perhaps some explanation for the elder Roper's desire to do this is that out of the ten children he fathered, only Robert had survived. The others died in "the Spring of life," as one account put it, and "their sorrowing and broken-hearted mother" soon followed them to her grave. Such things were commonplace in the early nineteenth century and may have suggested to the Roper patriarch that charity—not progeny—was the most reliable road to immortality.

The younger Roper, nevertheless, looked to architecture for his own lasting monument. For a man known in society as a penny-pincher, he built a house whose every feature speaks of generosity. The entrance hall is a grand space with a wide staircase designed for dramatic effect. Any visitor, even today, would expect to be admitted to such a hallway by a liveried servant and to surrender his walking stick, topcoat, and silk hat to the parlor maid. To the left is the entrance to a reception room with a glittering chandelier. Parquet floors and black marble mantelpieces gleam. Beyond the reception room is a formal dining room of imperial dimensions. Glass doors open into the garden, at the bottom of which sits a small teahouse. Out in the hallway the staircase curves invitingly into the upper stories, for this is not a house that resigns its public role at the top of the stairs, but begins it there.

The second floor, the piano nobile, has two drawing rooms, each with side openings to the five-columned portico, which in fine weather functioned as an adjunct to the rooms: a terrace, secluded well above the cobblestone street, cooled by ocean breezes and with the view almost to the coast of Africa. These drawing rooms were never intended as a cozy family hideaway, no place to sit and read the Bible or *Pilgrim's Progress*, or stitch a sampler, or enjoy an amateur musicale. These are rooms for state occasions, balls, brandy and cigars, receptions. Though the furnishings the Ropers used have disappeared without a trace, the showy, priceless, museum-quality antiques assembled by the present owner (more typical of nineteenth-century New York City than of Charleston) look very much at home in these rooms.

The floor plan of the house, with its sidehall feature, creates an interior very different from the smaller houses of an earlier Charleston. Though they too have their dining rooms and drawing rooms quite fit for grand occasions, the many purposes of the houses, their serviceability, are implicit in the design. In the

In the large front drawing room on the second floor, a portrait of George Washington by Charles Peale Polk hangs over the mantel above a gilded bronze clock, made in France during the early nineteenth century. The furnishings are by Duncan Phyfe, the well-known American cabinetmaker.

Overleaf: In another detail of the front drawing room, a second Duncan Phyfe couch stands against the wall at right. This one, a classic example of Empire style, features curule legs copied from a Roman campstool. The portrait, by Jeremiah Theus, is of Mrs. Thomas Grimball, who lived in Charleston in the eighteenth century.

Nathaniel Russell house (Chapter Three), for example, the visitor comes through the front door into a room, not a hallway. The staircase, quite as spectacular as the one in Roper House, sits farther back inside the dwelling, concealed from the eyes of the casual caller. This is not surprising in a house where the ground floor served as a place of business, with a room or rooms where a gentleman-merchant and a ship's captain might sit down with their ledgers. Roper House is definitely not commercial. It was not built for utility or convenience, or the nurturing of simple domestic values, but instead, for display.

Sadly, the house never quite fulfilled its purpose, at least so far as anybody knows. The Ropers often entertained, but "I have seen an entertainment which cost him several hundred dollars, go off rather badly because he was unwilling to spend ten or fifteen additional in order to have everything in keeping," a reproving friend relates. And soon, apparently without ever having lived up to the requirements of his own house, poor Roper died. Accounts of his death differ, but in 1842 or 1844 or 1845 "country fever" carried him off, and the estate went to found the hospital that still serves the city of Charleston. Martha Laurens Roper sold the house in 1851 to the Alston family, who resold it to the Ravenels; it has changed hands many times since.

Mrs. Roper lived until 1868, three years past the end of the Civil War, and she may have known of the near disaster that befell her former mansion. In the spring of 1865, when Charleston fell to the Federal onslaught, Confederate forces, aware that their guns were about to fall into enemy hands, blew up a thirty-eight-ton cannon in its emplacement close to the Roper house. A huge metal fragment landed on the roof and crashed through to the rafters, where it remains to this day, a conversation piece and a reminder of an era that met an abrupt and brutal end.

Opposite: The Duncan Phyfe Grecian couch here (and in another view on the preceding pages) has claw feet and blue silk uphostery. The pier table behind it, with Grecian motifs, and the exterior wrought-iron balcony together create a harmonious backdrop.

Overleaf: The west end of the double drawing room upstairs is filled with furnishings imported from New York, most notably a card table (center) by Joseph Meeks and the sofa and small side chairs, attributed to Duncan Phyfe. The gaslight chandelier is one of several made for the principal rooms of the house.

OUTLYING EDENS

Throughout the Colonial era the plantations on which the economy of Charleston depended maintained the finest gardens in America. The planters lavished extra care on the houses they built in town, which would be seen by a wider audience, but they reserved their best horticultural efforts for their countryseats. The first plantation gardens were made up primarily of nonflowering plants and shrubs, laid out in geometric patterns copied from the courts of Europe. In the late eighteenth and early nineteenth centuries, new plants such as the azalea and camellia introduced extravagant displays of color, and formal design gave way to casual luxuriance.

Two of the gardens on the following pages were created before the Revolution, and the first of these, Middleton Place (opposite and pages 162–163), is the oldest landscaped garden in America. In 1740 Henry Middleton sent to England for a gardener to design his estate on the Ashley River, and according to legend one hundred slaves labored ten years to create his vision of terraces, walks, and ponds. A few miles to the south is Magnolia Gardens (pages 164–167), largely the work of John Grimké Drayton, a minister who acted as his own landscape architect. Cypress Gardens (pages 168–171), on the Cooper River, was created in its present form in the early years of this century, but against a backdrop of venerable cypress trees and abandoned rice pools of a much earlier time. All three gardens are laid out in a setting so lush that, as one writer noted of Middleton Place, "no man may say just where man's garden ends and God's begins."

Middleton Place. *A live oak arches over Rice Mill Pond against a brilliant background of azaleas and white Cherokee roses. Penny weed and gator weed grow at the surface of the pond.*

Every spring at Middleton Place some thirty-five thousand azaleas blanket the hillside bordering the pond. The

first azaleas were introduced on the plantation in the 1840s; these were planted early in this century.

Magnolia Gardens. *Live oaks draped in wisteria vines give the garden a primeval air that is only partly dispelled*

by the neatly painted bridge. Built in the 1840s, the bridge spans a lake created by deepening a rice field.

Just across the bridge, daffodils bloom in St. Francis's Garden, which was named for the saint whose statue stands among the live oaks.

The still water of the lake mirrors the live oak trees as well as the pink and white azaleas planted on its banks. Dogwoods bloom in the distance.

Cypress Gardens. *In a clearing in a grove of sweet gum and pine, wisteria blossoms in its delicate lavender color.*

At center left is the fan-shaped palmetto that gives the landscape around Charleston its exotic air.

Rising out of the swamp that was once a rice field are the flared trunks of cypress trees, some of them thought to be two hundred years old. Just visible on the far bank is an azalea path that leads to an island in the swamp.

At the water's edge white atamasco lilies and pink azaleas bloom among the cypress knees—vertical anchors that grow from the roots of the trees to provide air and support to the root system.

Acknowledgments

The Editors are particularly grateful to the following people for their extensive assistance and cooperation: Henry Cauthen, Preservation Society of Charleston; J. Thomas Savage, curator, Historic Charleston Foundation; Frankie H. Webb, curator of historic houses, Charleston Museum; Anne Whitelaw; Mrs. Robert N.S. Whitelaw, consultant, Historic Charleston Foundation.

The Editors would also like to thank the following for their assistance: Mrs. Nathaniel I. Ball III, Edmondston-Alston House; Victor Barrett; Mr. and Mrs. Thomas R. Bennett, Pineapple House; David Richmond Byers III; Jane Colihan; Thomas Dickey; Barbara Doyle, secretary for the associates, Middleton Place Foundation; Mr. and Mrs. Charles Duell, Edmondston-Alston House and Middleton Plantation; Mrs. S. Henry Edmunds, director, Historic Charleston Foundation; Elizabeth Fitten, Heyward-Washington House; Anne Fox, Manigault House; W.E. Freeman, director, Charleston Museum; Richard H. Jenrette, Roper House; Kenneth Jones, curator of decorative arts, Charleston Museum; Sarah Lytle, director, Middleton Place Foundation; Sabra Moore; Mr. and Mrs. Charles Paul; Mrs. Frances J. Pelzer III, director, Historic Charleston Reproductions; Raymond L. Porfilio, Jr.; Susan Quattlebaum, public information coordinator, Mayor's Office, Charleston; Evelyn Raskopf, New-York Historical Society; Miki Schneider, Manigault House; Mrs. Benjamin B. Smith, Edmondston-Alston House; Anne Thomas, Manigault House; Candice Wilkin, Historic Charleston Foundation; Mr. and Mrs. Joseph Young, Robert Pringle House.

Credits

Cover and all pages except those noted below are by Peter Vitale. Page 7: Steven Mays. 8: Library of Congress. 9: Mabel Brady Garvan Collection, Yale University Art Gallery. 10: Courtesy National Trust for Historic Preservation. 11: Abby Aldrich Rockefeller Folk Art Center, Williamsburg, Virginia. 12–14: Steven Mays. 15: Carl Guttenberger. 16: Courtesy American Antiquarian Society. 17: Collection of City Hall, Charleston; Terry Richardson. 19: Independence National Historical Park Collection. 27: The South Carolina Historical Society. 38: Steven Mays. 39: Carl Guttenberger. 40–41: Steven Mays. 42: Carl Guttenberger. 43 (top): Steven Mays. 43 (bottom): Carl Guttenberger. 44–45: Steven Mays. 46–47: Carl Guttenberger. 48–49: Steven Mays. 52: Collection of Carolina Art Association, Gibbes Art Gallery. 55: Courtesy The Henry Francis du Pont Winterthur Museum. 65: Steven Mays. 69: Steven Mays/Charleston Museum. 70–71: Steven Mays/Middleton Place. 72–79: Steven Mays/Edmondston-Alston House, Historic Charleston Foundation. 80–81: High Museum of Art. 83: Steven Mays. 85: Historic Charleston Foundation. 97: Collection of Carolina Art Association, Gibbes Art Gallery. 101: Terry Richardson, Historic Charleston Foundation. 103–107: Steven Mays/Heyward-Washington House. 108: Steven Mays/Middleton Place. 109: Steven Mays/Nathaniel Russell House, Historic Charleston Foundation. 110–112: Steven Mays/Heyward-Washington House. 113: Steven Mays/Middleton Place. 114–115: Steven Mays/Heyward-Washington House. 117: Carl Guttenberger. 126: Historic Charleston Foundation. 129–139: The New-York Historical Society. 140–141: John Wallen/Art, Prints, and Photographs Division, New York Public Library. 150: Prints Division, New York Public Library. 151: Collection of Carolina Art Association, Gibbes Art Gallery. 161–171: Derek Fell.

Index

Page numbers set in *italic* refer to captions.

abolitionist movement, 33
Adam, Robert, 15–16, 55, 85
Adamesque architecture, 15–16
   of Manigault House, *51*
Adamesque design, 55, *55*
   in Russell House, 85, *93*
Albani, Francesco, *89*
Allston, Robert F.W., 97
Alston, Charles, *116*, 119–126
   silver of, *73, 74*
Alston, Charles, Jr., 121
Alston, Emma Pringle, 121–124
Alston, John Julius, 121, 126
Alston, Joseph, 121, 124
Alston, Susan, 121–126
Alston, William, 119–121
   silver of, *76*
Alston family, 121, 124
   Roper House bought by, 157
   silver of, *73–79*
American Empire style, *144*
American Revolution, 16, 19, 150
   Heyward in, 24
   Manigault family in, 62
   Middleton family in, 93
architecture
   Adamesque, 15–16
   of Charleston houses, 12–13
   of Colonial Charleston, 15
   of Edmondston-Alston House, *116*
   of entrances, *36–49*
   Georgian, 7, 15
   Greek Revival, 143–144
   of Heyward-Washington House, 19–21, 24
   of historic Charleston houses, 8–9
   of Manigault House, 51–55, *51, 52*
   of Roper House, 152
   of Russell House, 83–85
   of Single House, 11–12, *14*
art
   of Audubon, *128–141*
   of Charleston silver, 68–81
   created by slaves, 14
   of Elfe's woodcarvings, *21, 24, 24, 29*
Ashley Cooper, Lord Anthony (earl of Shaftesbury), 10
Ashley River, 7, *8, 160*
Audubon, John, *135*
Audubon, John James, 124, *128–141*

Bachman, John *128, 130*
Baily & Company (silversmiths), *73*
Bateman, Hester, *76*
Battery, The, 150, *150*
Beauregard, P.G.T., 124–126
birds, Audubon's paintings of, *128–141*
Birds of America, The (Audubon), *128, 140–141*
Black-Crowned Night Heron (painting, Audubon), *132–133*
Blacklock House, *36, 43*
blacks
   art of, 14
   as slaves, *11*   *see also* slavery and slaves
Blue Crane, or Heron (painting, Audubon), *131*
bookcases, *103–107, 114*
bowls, silver, *68–81*
Boyce (silversmiths), *55*
Brewton (Miles) House, 7, 15, 16, *48–49*, 119
Broad Street, 51

Calhoun, John C., 150–151
Carolina Low Country, 13, 14, *130*
cast-iron gates, *36*
Castle Pinckey, *129*
chairs, *110*
   Chippendale, *97*
   by Elfe, *115*
Charles II (king, England), 9
Charleston
   American Revolution, in 24
   architectural styles in, 11–13, 143–144
   Audubon in, *128*
   Civil War in, 17, 124–126
   Colonial, 9–11, 15
   decline of, 147
   entrances to houses in, *36–49*
   founded by aristocratic families, 83
   furniture of, *102–115*
   gardens of, *160–171*
   historic district of, 7–8
   Huguenot settlers in, 59
   lives of women in, 93–100
   as settlement, *8*
   silver of, *68–81*
   streets of, 7
   in War of 1812, 150
   G. Washington in, 29
Charleston Museum, 8, 24
   Ewan silver in, *69*
   Heyward-Washington House bought by, 33
   Manigault House owned by, 62–65
chevaux de frise iron gates, *48–49*
Chippendale, Thomas, *102*
Chippendale furniture
   chairs, *110*
   Elfe table in style of, *108*
   in Heyward-Washington House, *21*
Church Street, 19, 21
city hall (Charleston), 52
Civil War, 17, 124–126, 151, *151,* 157
Clapper Rail (painting, Audubon), *139*

173

Clay, Henry, *144*
Clinton, Sir Henry, 16
Colonial architecture, 143–144
Colonial Charleston, 9–11, 15
Colonial furniture, *103–107*
Columbia (South Carolina), 17
columns, *93, 116,* 144, 147
Confederate Museum, 8
Continental Congresses, 24
Cooper River, 7, *8,* 29
    Cypress Gardens on, *160*
Corinthian columns, *93, 116,* 144
Cornwallis, Charles, 27
couches
    Phyfe, *153, 157*
    Récamier, *93, 147*
Cypress Gardens, *160, 168–171*

Declaration of Independence, 27
Dehon, Sarah Russell, 93, 97
Dehon, Theodore, 93
Dock Street Theater, *42, 45*
doors, *36–49*
Doric columns, *116*
Double House, 12
Drayton, Charlotte (Manigault), 52, 62
Drayton, John Grimké, *160*
Drayton Hall, *10,* 97

earthquakes, 13, 17
East Battery, *9*
economy
    of Charleston of 1830s, 144
    of Colonial Charleston, *10,* 11
    cotton in, 119
    silver in, 68
    slavery in, 13, 14, *16*
Edmondston, Charles, 116–119

Edmondston-Alston House, 116–126, *116*
    dining room in, *121*
    drawing room in, *121*
    library in, *126*
    piazza in, *124*
    silver in, *73*
    staircase in, *119*
18 Bull Street (Blacklock House), *36, 43*
8 Legare Street, *44*
87 Church Street, *see* Heyward-Washington House
Elfe, Thomas, 21, 24, *24,* 29, 102
    chair by, *115*
    chest by, *112*
    table by, *108*
emblems, *12*
Empire-style furniture, *126, 144, 153*
Empire-style silver, *70*
English Regency furniture, *147*
entrances, *36–49*
    to Manigault House, *59*
    to Roper House, *147*
    to Russell House, *83*
Erard, Sébastien, 93
Eveleigh, George, 15
Ewan, John, 68–70

Female Domestic Missionary Society, 97
feminist movement, 33
54 Meeting Street, *40–41*
51 Meeting Street, *see* Russell (Nathaniel) House
fires, 12, *12,* 16–17, *17*
Five Woodpeckers (painting, Audubon), *134*
Fort Sumter, 124–126, 150, *151*
14 Legare Street, *38*
France, 59
Fraser, Charles, *19*
French Empire furniture, *147*

Friesland (Netherlands), *48–49*
furniture, *102–115*
    Chippendale, *21*
    in Edmondston-Alston House, *121, 126*
    Elfe bed, *29*
    in Manigault House, *55, 63, 65*
    in Roper House, *147, 157*
    in Russell House, *89, 93, 97*

gardens, *160–171*
    for Heyward-Washington House, 33
    for Roper House, 152
    for Russell House, 93
gates (entrances), *36–49*
George I furniture, *97*
Georges (kings, England), 15
Georgian architecture, 7, 15
    entrances, *36*
    of Heyward-Washington House, 24
Giton, Judith (Manigault), 59–65
Greco-Roman architecture, 7, 15, 16
Greek Revival architecture, *116,* 121
    of Roper House, 143
Greek style of furniture, *157*
Grimball, Mrs. Thomas, *153*
Grimké, Angelina, 30–33
Grimké, John, 30
Grimké, Sarah, *19,* 30–33

harps, *93*
Havell, Robert, *131*
headright system of land distribution, 10
Henry IV (king, France), 59
Hepplewhite, George, *102*
Hepplewhite furniture, *89, 110*
Heyward, Daniel, *21,* 24, 29
Heyward, Elizabeth, 29

Heyward, Elizabeth Matthewes, 24, 27, 33
Heyward, Thomas, 19, *19*, 24–33, *27, 29*
Heyward-Washington House, 19–33, *19*
  dining room of, *21*
  drawing room of, *21*
  Elfe bed in, *29*
  furniture in, *102*
  kitchen for, *30, 33*
Historic Charleston Foundation, 100
Hopton, Sarah (Russell), 89, 97
Houdon, Jean Antoine, *147*
houses
  architecture of, 12–13
  of East Battery, *9*
  Edmondston-Alston, 116–126
  entrances to, 36–49
  Eveleigh's, *15*
  gardens of, *160–171*
  Georgian, *7, 15*
  Heyward-Washington, 19–33
  of historic Charleston, 8–9
  Manigault, 51–65
  Roper, 143–157
  Russell, 83–100
  Single, 11–12
Huguenots, 55–59
hurricanes, *13*, 17

immigration, to Colonial Charleston, 10
ironwork
  of Edmondston-Alston House balcony, *116*
  gates of, *36, 44–49*

Jefferson, Thomas, 27, 52, 144
Johnson, Samuel, 13
Jones, Inigo, 13
Joseph Meeks & Sons (furniture makers), *147*

kitchen, for Heyward-Washington House, *30, 33*

Lafayette, Marquis Marie de, *147*
Laurens, Martha Rutledge (Roper), 151, 157
Lehman, George, *129, 130*
Lewis and Clark expedition, *136*
library, in Edmondston-Alston House, 121, 124, *126*
Locke, John, 10
Long-Billed Curlew (painting, Audubon), *129*
Louis XIV (king, France), 59
Louis XV furniture, *65*
Low Country, 13, 14, *130*

Magnolia Gardens, *160, 164–167*
Manigault, Charlotte Drayton, 52, 62
Manigault, Charles, *65*
Manigault, Gabriel, 51–52, *51, 52, 59*, 62, 65
Manigault, Gabriel (grandfather), 62
Manigault, Joseph, 52, *59*, 62
Manigault, Judith Giton, 59–65
Manigault, Maria Middleton, 52
Manigault, Peter, *55*
Manigault, Pierre, 59–65
Manigault family, 55–59
Manigault House, 51–65, *51, 52*
  bedroom in, *63*
  central hall and staircase in, *59*
  furnishings in, *55, 59, 65*
Matthewes, Elizabeth (Heyward), 24, 27, 33
Mayr, Christian, *17*
Meeks, Joseph, *147, 157*

Meeting Street, 8
Middleton, Alicia Russell, 89–93
Middleton, Arthur, 89–93, 97
Middleton, Henry, *160*
Middleton, Maria (Manigault), 52
Middleton, Thomas, 97
Middleton family, 93
Middleton Place, *108, 112*
  garden of, *160–162*
mirrors, *21*
music, 97
  Erard harp, *93*
  of slaves, *11*
  spinet, *27*

Nathaniel Russell House, *see* Russell (Nathaniel) House
neoclassical silversmithing, *76, 78*
9 East Battery, *see* Roper House

One East Battery, *37*
116 Broad Street, *46–47*

Palladian windows, 55
Phyfe, Duncan, *153, 157*
pianos, 27
piazzas, 9, 11, 13
  in Edmondston-Alston House, 116, *116, 124*
  in Eveleigh's House, *15*
  in Manigault House, 51
  in Pringle House, *14*
  in Roper House, *143*, 147, *147–150*
plantations, *10*, 11
  slaves on, *11, 14*
Polk, Charles Peale, *153*
porcelain, *121*
Pringle, Emma (Alston), 121–124
Pringle House, *14*

Quadrupeds (Audubon), 124

Race Week, 124
Ravenel family, 157
Récamier couches, *93, 147*
Red-Breasted Merganser (painting, Audubon), *140–141*
Regency silver, *78*
religion, 10, 55–59
Rice Mill Pond, *161*
Richmond (Virginia), 17
Robertson, Walter, *52*
Rococo furniture, *110*
Roman architecture, 16, 143, 144
Romney, George, *85*
Roper, Martha Rutledge Laurens, 151, 157
Roper, Robert William, 143, 150–157
Roper, William, 121
Roper family, 152
Roper House, 143–157, *143, 150*
   damaged in Civil War, *151*
   dining room of, *144*
   drawing rooms of, *153, 157*
   reception room of, *147*
Russell, Alicia (Middleton), 89–93
Russell, Nathaniel, 83, *85*, 89–93, 100
Russell, Sarah (Dehon), 89, 93, 97
Russell, Sarah Hopton, 89, 97
Russell (Nathaniel) House, 16, 83–100, *83, 100*
   bedroom in, *97*
   entrance to, *42*, 157
   furniture in, *109*
   oval room in, *97*
   staircase in, 55, *85*

Sage Grouse (painting, Audubon), *136–137*
Saint Augustine (Florida), 27

St. Francis's Garden, *166*
St. Michael's Episcopal Church, 8, *27*, 93
Sherman, William T., 17
silver, *68–81*
   in Edmondston-Alston House, *121*
   in Manigault House, *55*
   in Roper House, *144*
Single House, 11–12, *14*
Sisters of Charity of Our Lady of Mercy, 97
slavery and slaves, 10, *11*, 13–14, *16*, 121, 151
   Grimké sisters' opposition to, 30–33
   Middleton garden created by, *160*
   in volunteer fire department, *17*
Smith, Mary Rutledge, *85*
Snowy Egret (painting, Audubon), *130*
South Carolina
   Civil War in, 17
   in Revolutionary War, 16
South Carolina Historical Society, 121
South Carolina Society Hall, 52
staircases
   in Edmondston-Alston House, *119*
   in Manigault House, 55, *59*
   in Roper House, *144*, 152
   in Russell House, 16, 85, *85*, 89–93, 157
Storr, Paul, *55*
Swainson's Hawk (painting, Audubon), *138*

tableware, silver, *68–81*
   in Manigault House, *55*
Theus, Jeremiah, *19, 21, 153*
350 Meeting Street, *see* Manigault House

21 East Battery, *see* Edmondston-Alston House
26 Battery, *39*

Villa Margherita, *44*

Warblers and Bluebirds (painting, Audubon), *135*
War of 1812, 150
Washington, George, *19*, 27, *153*
   at Heyward-Washington House, 29
Weld, Theodore, 33
Wilmot, Samuel, *81*
women, 27–29, 59
   in Charleston society, 93–100
   S. Grimké on, 33
woodworking, *102*
   Adamesque, *93*
   by Elfe, *21*, 24, *24*, 29